# A Working Faith
# in an Age of Science

science and religion in harmony

Ken Dutton

Hemhill Books

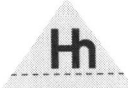

Published by
Hemhill Books
website: www.hemhillbooks.com
e-mail: admin@hemhillbooks.com

Copyright © Ken Dutton, 2014
The author welcomes any comments or queries via the publisher, or directly via his website:
www.kendutton.com

The moral right of Ken Dutton to be identified as the author of this work has been asserted in accordance with the
Copyright, Design and Patents Act, 1988.

All rights reserved. No part of this publication may be reproduced or transmitted in any form or by any means, electronic or mechanical, including photocopying, recording, or by any information storage and retrieval system, without permission in writing from the publisher.

Front cover images from photographs provided by the author.
Back cover background from a watercolour by Hilary Bradley.

Scripture quotations taken from THE HOLY BIBLE, NEW INTERNATIONAL VERSION. Copyright © 1973, 1978, 1984
by International Bible Society. Used by permission.

British Library Cataloguing-in-Publication Data
A catalogue record for this book is available from
the British Library.

ISBN 978-0-9929659-0-7

*To*

*Lizzie, Suzie and Katie*

*With love*

# Contents

| | |
|---|---|
| Contents | v |
| Acknowledgements | vii |
| Introduction – Interesting Questions | ix |
|    A few questions | x |
|    About this book | xii |
|    About the Author | xv |
| Chapter 1  Science and Religion – What's the Problem? | 1 |
|    Conflict or harmony? | 2 |
|    What is the scientific method? | 4 |
|    Faith and science | 7 |
|    Different types of explanation | 11 |
| Chapter 2  Science and Religion – Some Wider Issues | 15 |
|    What is the problem with proof? | 15 |
|    Nothing buttery | 19 |
|    Where is the god of the gaps? | 22 |
|    Surely it's not all intellectual? | 24 |
|    Moving on | 27 |
| Chapter 3  Uncertainty and Unpredictability | 29 |
|    Does the universe run like clockwork? | 29 |
|    Uncertainty | 33 |
|    Unpredictability | 34 |
|    Why does this matter? | 39 |
| Chapter 4  Creation | 41 |
|    How did we arrive at 21st century science? | 41 |
|    In the beginning – why the 'big bang' idea? | 43 |
|    What other evidence is there for the big bang? | 47 |
|    What happened in the very early universe? | 49 |
|    The proportion of helium in the universe | 50 |
|    The cosmic microwave background radiation | 52 |
|    Religious aspects of the big bang | 53 |
| Chapter 5  The Structure of the Universe | 55 |
|    Where did the stars come from? | 59 |

| | |
|---|---|
| How many stars? | 61 |
| The lives of the stars | 64 |
| How was the carbon for life formed? | 66 |

### Chapter 6  The Evolution of Life — 71
| | |
|---|---|
| Cells, genetics and DNA | 75 |
| Towards the origin of life? | 83 |
| Intelligent design? | 86 |

### Chapter 7  Science, the Bible and Morals — 91
| | |
|---|---|
| How do science and Genesis compare? | 95 |
| Is that the best approach? | 97 |
| What does Christ have to do with creation? | 100 |
| The moral law | 104 |

### Chapter 8  What is the Fine-Tuning of the Universe? — 111
| | |
|---|---|
| What does "fine-tuning" mean? | 111 |
| Are simple explanations enough? | 113 |

### Chapter 9  A Few Examples of Fine-Tuning — 119
| | |
|---|---|
| The Goldilocks zone | 120 |
| The existence of carbon | 122 |
| The forces of gravity and electromagnetism | 123 |
| The strength of the strong nuclear force | 124 |
| Dark matter and dark energy | 125 |
| The smoothness of the universe | 128 |
| The masses of the proton and neutron | 129 |
| What can we conclude from this? | 129 |

### Chapter 10  Free Will and Free World — 131
| | |
|---|---|
| What does God have to do with free will? | 134 |
| Does the universe make itself? | 137 |

### Chapter 11  Does God Act in the World? — 145
| | |
|---|---|
| Prayer | 145 |
| How might God be able to act? | 149 |
| Miracles | 156 |
| Non-obvious actions of God | 159 |

### Chapter 12  Drawing it All Together — 163
| | |
|---|---|
| Drawing it all together | 166 |

| | |
|---|---|
| Endnotes | 171 |
| Index | 187 |

# Acknowledgements

For more than 45 years I have been helped by the writings of a large number of authors, of various persuasions. Whenever I refer to their work, I accept full responsibility for my interpretation of it, and for omitting their closely reasoned supporting arguments, in order to keep this book suitable for a general readership. Those writers have all gone about their tasks much more rigorously than some of my brief interpretations might suggest.

I am extremely grateful to my wife, Liz, who didn't expect me to spend so much time producing another book immediately after I had 'retired'. She has supported me throughout, and is always a source of love, affection, good humor and good sense. Many others of my family and friends have been consistently helpful and encouraging during the writing of this book, and I thank them too – you know who you are.

Finally, special thanks go to those who gave up their time to make helpful comments about various aspects of the book: Ian Bell, Liz Dutton, Naomi Gordon, Tim Hanstock, Iris Harris, Zoë Hobson, Alison Hull, Rob Keen, Jane Pettinger, Mick Rolley and David Wilkinson. Four of these good folk were kind enough to provide comments on the entire manuscript.

As a result of the various suggestions, the book is at least 33 percent shorter than the original draft, and much more readable. I ignored some perfectly valid suggestions though, so the responsibility for any shortcomings in the final result rests firmly with me.

I am happy to receive any comments via my website at
www.kendutton.com

Ken Dutton
Sheffield,
July 2014

## Introduction – Interesting Questions

Since you have picked up this book, you are probably interested in the relationship between science and religion. Excellent! Those two areas of knowledge have perhaps had a greater influence than anything else on the development of our modern societies.

Both science and religion have valuable things to say about the universe and our place in it, but in order fully to appreciate the relationship between them and the contribution that each can make, it is necessary to have a significant level of knowledge in both areas. Starting on the next page is a list of interesting questions, which demonstrates this requirement quite well.

To someone who knows a lot of science, but relatively little about religion, religion can seem distant from her every-day world, perhaps even completely irrelevant. Occasionally though, it might get uncomfortably close – at those times when religion is blamed for wars and terrorist attacks, for example.

On the other hand, if someone has a religious faith, but is not particularly well informed about scientific matters, the world of science and technology might seem a threatening, unapproachable place in which to try to explain his religious views. Incidentally, I don't like the words 'religion' and 'religious', but the reasons for that can wait until later.

It took me many years to satisfy myself that there need be no real disagreements between science and religion, and that I could hold an authentic religious faith at the same time as being a professional scientist. This book will have fulfilled its purpose if it helps you to learn something new about the relationship between science and religion, in a much shorter timescale than it has taken me.

This Introduction ends with a short section containing a little about my qualifications for writing the book but, before that, here's an introduction to some of the things we shall be considering later.

Note that superscripts in text, such as this[1], refer to the notes at the end of the book and can be ignored if you wish. On the other hand superscripts in numbers, which you might know as 'powers' (as in $10^3$) are a different matter; they will be explained later.

## A few questions

Over many years I have given occasional talks to various groups about the relationship between science and religion. Both the talks themselves, and the question-and-answer sessions after the talks, have covered some fascinating questions.

The idea for this book arose from the desire to present some of the material from my talks, and listeners' questions, which might be helpful to a wider audience.

There follows a list of some of the interesting questions considered later in the book:

- How do scientists actually go about their work?
- What are the limitations of the scientific approach?
- What different types of explanation might there be for any given situation? For example, is the kettle boiling because of heat energy being transferred to the water from the heating element, which has an electric current flowing though it? Or is it boiling because I want a hot drink? If you've not come across this illustration before, note that the 'scientific' explanation is about the mechanisms and processes, whereas the alternative explanation is about the purpose, or intention involved. Neither of the two explanations needs to make any reference to the other; both are correct, and both are necessary for a full understanding of the situation.
- How should the writings in ancient holy books be interpreted? Our present scientific method of analyzing things didn't emerge until the sixteenth and seventeenth centuries, so it seems illogical to interpret them as modern science texts. Perhaps they are more about the second type of explanation in the previous paragraph – more concerned with purposes than with mechanisms and processes. Could those purposes lie in the Mind of God?
- What do religious people actually believe? The media in general, and overtly atheistic writers and broadcasters in particular, tend to propagate caricatures of religious belief and behavior. Ill-informed caricatures of religion, or even deliberately misleading ones, bear

little relationship to the genuine article and are easy targets; the real thing is not so easy to dismiss.
- How does the scientific view of the creation of the universe relate to the religious view that God created it, and that he[2] holds it in being from moment to moment?
- Why do most scientists think that the universe is about 13.7 billion years old? If you think that it is of a different age, what are the consequences of believing that?
- Is evolution, as built on the ideas of Mendel and Darwin, a good scientific theory? If so, what are the consequences for holding other views?
- Even though Genesis (the first book of the Jewish and Christian scriptures) is not a science text, how well does its bronze-age creation account stack up against our best scientific descriptions?
- Assuming that God exists, if he is all-loving and all-powerful, why is there so much suffering in the world?
- Does God answer prayers, or can it always be put down to coincidence?
- If God does answer prayers, are there any that he cannot answer? If there are, where does that leave the idea that he is all-powerful?
- If God is all knowing, is he perhaps a bit incompetent too, given that the world sometimes seems to be in such a mess?
- Christianity suggests that you and I can have personal relationships with God. However, given the scale of the universe, it seems that we might have appeared by chance, on an insignificant speck of dust, orbiting a star which is only one of at least 200 billion stars in our galaxy (that's two hundred thousand million). Our galaxy is then only one of perhaps 100 billion galaxies, in a universe that, some suggest, is only one of a vast number of universes. So why on Earth should God care about us?
- Why is it that the laws of nature seem to have 'already' been built into the universe at the instant of creation – where did they come from?
- Why is it that the fixed numbers which we use in those laws of nature (such as the speed of light, and the gravitational constant) seem to have 'already' been in existence when the universe was created – where did they come from?
- Why is it that we can apply the laws of nature at any time and in any place and get the same results?
- Given that the laws of nature are so regular, if God exists is he able actually to do anything by way of directly acting in the universe?

For example, can he grant miraculous answers to prayer? If he is able to do such things, how is it that we can actually discover those consistently regular laws of nature at all? Instead, shouldn't we be experiencing a chaotic series of unpredictable miracles, making science impossible because there would be no regular, repeatable patterns of behavior to be observed?
- If we assume that God has given us free will to make our own choices in life, can he act without infringing the free will he has given?
- Why would a supposedly loving God create hell, and then allow some (presumably bad) people to be born, knowing that they would be condemned to spend eternity there?
- Would you have to disengage your brain in order to be able to believe in a god?

## About this book

There are many good books available that would help in answering the questions in the previous section. However, I have not seen one that compares favorably with this book in *all* of the following aspects:
- The author has been both a highly qualified professional scientist, and an active Christian, for almost 40 years.
- The author is a chartered engineer – and the uniquely pragmatic approach of the engineer is evident throughout the book.
- You don't need a degree to understand this book. Specialist technical words are avoided where possible, and explained where they cannot be avoided.
- There are very few books which cover everything mentioned in this one, and even fewer that do so in an introductory manner using non-specialist language.
- There is more explanation of the scientific aspects in this book, than in most others in this area. The science is covered in a 'popular science' style, in keeping with the book's introductory ethos.
- The best of the competitive books tend to be much more expensive than this one.

There is a wide range of views about the relationship between science and religion. In my late-teenage years, my own viewpoint might have been summarized as, 'fairly knowledgeable about science, sympathetic to religion, but unable to match the two together – and, as a result, tending to stick with the science'.

Within the more fundamentalist reaches of religion, there are those who will not accept scientific results, however well researched they may be, if the science seems to contradict their religion. In science, there are some who could also be called fundamentalists. They claim that anything worth knowing can be explained by the methods of science; if something cannot be scientifically tested, it is considered to be of little value. Religion, to such people, simply looks like outdated superstition, left over from a less-enlightened age.

Both those sets of people, and those of many shades of opinion in between, can benefit from considering the questions posed in the previous section. In looking at questions that arise at the interface between science and religion, this book seeks to foster mutual understanding between those two ways of viewing the universe and our place in it.

In doing so it presents details of sufficient science to ensure that less-scientific readers can gain an understanding of how science works, what its limitations are, and why its properly researched results must be taken seriously.

In parallel, it describes how religious ideas can sit side-by-side with the modern scientific results. It explains that the existence of God can never be logically proved or disproved, and that therefore we can each decide for ourselves whether God might be, in fact, the best explanation for the way some things seem to be.

The book acknowledges the tendency of some religious people to use God as an explanation for anything they don't understand, but it also demonstrates that such gaps in our knowledge have often been closed as our scientific understanding has advanced. It therefore advises against that kind of approach.

Instead, it emphasizes some of the areas where religion can contribute to our knowledge using the types of explanation which science cannot offer, because of science's self-limitation of the types of problem it can address. This section ends with a brief summary of the structure of the book.

The book was written with the intention that it would be read from front to back, in sequence. However, some parts may occasionally go a bit too deeply into the science for some readers. In such cases, as you read, there are suggestions as to where you may skip material if you wish, though you may miss something important if you do. The following chapter summaries indicate what you will find in each chapter, and therefore what you might miss if you read the chapters out of sequence.

The first two chapters are introductory, and include more detail about several of the ideas we have already mentioned.

Chapter Three looks at two relatively recent ideas in science. As a result of these, we now know that it is impossible for science to generate a completely 'clockwork' description of the universe. This is important because, over the years, some scientists have always predicted that such a description would remove the need for God altogether; many people who are unaware of the material in Chapter Three still believe that. In fact, it turns out that we shall never be able accurately to predict how a lot of the systems we analyze will behave as they propagate into the future. As one specific example, these ideas indicate that accurate long-term weather forecasting will never become a reality. For some people, the type of information in this chapter makes it intellectually acceptable to consider that God might exist, and might be acting in the world in ways that do not compromise the findings of science.

Chapters four to six are largely presentations of the main, currently accepted, scientific ideas of creation and evolution. They constitute a mini popular-science introduction to the big bang theory, the formation of galaxies and stars, the nuclear reactions in stars that generate all the chemicals we need for life, the basic ideas behind evolutionary theories, and some of the workings of DNA, chromosomes and genes. As well as indicating how carefully science has gone about analyzing these areas, and how reliable the results are, these chapters also indicate some of the areas where science does not go, because they are unsuitable for scientific testing and analysis. Religious ideas can safely be proposed to fill this type of 'gap', as science will not close such gaps in the future. These ideas are complementary to the science, not competitive alternatives to it.

The first part of Chapter Seven looks at the apparent discrepancies between the first two chapters of Genesis (the first book of the Jewish and Christian scriptures) and the scientific ideas of creation and evolution. These have been a point of contention between some Christians and others for over 150 years. Although the overall view of this book is that Genesis was not intended to be a science text, the comparison between Genesis and science is an interesting one. The latter part of Chapter Seven considers the fact that we all seem to have an idea of what is right and wrong, and that the more fundamental parts of this knowledge seem to be independent of cultural influences.

Chapters eight and nine look at the fact that several unlikely coincidences must have occurred in order for Earth to exist, and for us to exist on it. Specific examples are given of some of these coincidences, which are unlikely to an extreme degree. The basic suggestion is that science can really only say that these are very unlikely coincidences, whereas religion can propose that God had a purpose for the universe and set things up accordingly. The attempts of some scientists to provide alternative answers seem at least as speculative as the God idea.

Chapter 10 looks at the notions that we have free will to choose what we shall do, and that the universe has freedom, in some sense, to 'make itself'. God is linked to both these ideas, and Chapter 11 goes on to consider how, if the ideas of Chapter 10 are correct, God might be able to act in the world without infringing those 'freedoms' that he is assumed to have given. There is also the problem of how God might be able to act without upsetting the regular workings of the universe on which the progress of science depends. In discussing these things, Chapter 11 also looks at how prayer and miracles fit into all of this.

Finally, Chapter 12 draws together the various threads that have run throughout the book. In discussing all the various matters outlined above, the book has been gradually gathering some of the pieces of evidence for the existence of God; Chapter 12 summarizes them.

## About the Author

Here's a little more about my background, to help you understand my approach and biases whilst you're reading.

From a very early age I displayed an excessive interest in all things scientific and technical. I always chose science and mathematics options at school, and my first degree is in a very technical area of engineering. I eventually achieved Chartered Engineer status, and was elected a Fellow of two of the United Kingdom's professional engineering institutions.

All this makes me very much an *applied* scientist, rather than a *pure* scientist such as a theoretical physicist. Everything I have designed, whilst working in industry, and as a consultant during my university career, has had to earn its keep. Unusually, I even carried out my PhD whilst working full-time in industry, because it fitted in with the research and development work I was doing on the automatic control of a difficult industrial process.

I spent 10 years as a research and development engineer in the steel industry, so I have a very pragmatic approach – my science has to work in the real world.

I have spent almost 30 years as a university lecturer, in a branch of engineering that some students can find difficult, and I co-wrote a major university textbook in that area. I am used to explaining complex things in straightforward language.

My pragmatic approach extends to my thinking about the relationship between science and religion. My religion also has to make sense in the real world, and there cannot be any contradiction between it, and my knowledge of science.

Because I am a Christian, there is an unavoidable Christian bias in the religious aspects of this book. Since I anticipate a predominantly 'western' readership, that doesn't necessarily matter. However, from my contact with people of other faiths, I know that many of the ideas will still be of interest to them. I have not set out overtly to preach Christianity in this book, but I do have to refer to it because it is the faith about which I am most knowledgeable.

I have attended a Christian church since birth, but I didn't feel able to take the step of becoming a Christian until the age of 22. The main reason for that was my knowledge of science in my mid- to late-teenage years.

At that time, it seemed to me that the predominant view in my church was that the universe had been created in six days, as suggested by a literal reading of the first two chapters of the Christian Bible. My knowledge of the 'big bang' theory of creation, for which I knew there was excellent scientific evidence, meant that I therefore found myself at odds with what I thought I was expected to believe in the church. To a lesser extent, the same applied to my knowledge of the scientific thinking on evolution.

Those problems were solved by starting to read books about the relationship between science and faith, rather than just the books about science that I had been reading ever since I was old enough to do so.

My hope is that the distillation of some of my reading, thinking and discussions, in this introductory book, will be of some help to you too.

# Chapter 1  Science and Religion –
## What's the Problem?

The chances are that you live in a society that is heavily reliant on technology. Science is ultimately responsible for its buildings, transport, communications, medical facilities, heating, lighting, water supply, and so on. Whether you are fascinated by the science, or just a grateful user of its benefits, you cannot escape it – it would only take a long-term failure of the electricity supply for a modern society to fall apart completely.[3]

In its purer forms, science has proved to be an excellent tool, not only for discovering the workings of the world in which we live, but also how we humans are put together, and even how the universe itself has evolved. Given that we live on an insignificant planet, totally lost in the immensity of the universe, that is a remarkable achievement. We shall look at some of the details later.

Unless someone really understands how science goes about its business, its success, and the all-pervading nature of technology, can lead to the belief that science can tell us all we need to know about the universe and our place in it.

I am as aware as anyone of the achievements of science, and its ability to explain the things mentioned above. However, in common with a large proportion of the world's population, I am also religious.

As a result, I am equally aware that I belong to a significant body of scientists, past and present, who have discovered that there is no contradiction between their science and their religious faith. Many of them are extremely well known, and a few of their names appear below.

The obvious question is, how can scientists, with all their implied traits of rational, analytical thought, also be believers in a supernatural god? And that's only the first question.

In any discussion about the relationship between science and religion, attention soon shifts to a whole range of questions that impinge on the possibility of that relationship being a harmonious one. Some of these are technical, some are more philosophical, but the serious investigator might eventually need to think about them all. Several of these interesting questions were listed in the Introduction to this book.

## Conflict or harmony?

Imagine that you have been given the task of arranging a debate between a scientist and a representative of religion. Whom will you choose to take part? The debate needs to be respectfully argued but, if those taking part are so respectful that they agree with each other on every point, it will become a boring non-event. To avoid that, you will almost certainly choose a non-religious scientist.

That's a sensible thing to do, but if you really want the sparks to fly you might go a step further and deliberately select a fundamentalist religious participant. The resulting 'discussion' might then give the impression that there is no possibility of agreement between the scientific and religious views of the universe, and that scientists cannot be religious believers. Neither of those things is true.

In fact, religious scientists such as Copernicus, Bacon, Kepler and Galileo, were largely responsible for the dawn of modern science in the sixteenth and seventeenth centuries. These were not scientists who just happened to be religious because most people were in those days; rather, they developed the science explicitly because they wanted to understand God's handiwork. For example, Kepler said that he was, "Thinking God's thoughts after him."

Religious scientists have contributed significantly to the progress of science ever since; they still do. A small selection of these, spanning the seventeenth to the twenty-first centuries, includes Boyle, Newton, Faraday, Maxwell, Kelvin, Eddington, Lemaître, Polkinghorne and Collins. Many of these men were also doing the science explicitly because of their religious beliefs. Several of them (including three of the four who lived in the twentieth and twenty first centuries) also held offices in the church, or chose to belong to non-mainstream Christian denominations. Such people are usually religious by deliberate choice, rather than simply by habit. Francis Collins, for example, was previously a self-confessed atheist.

The present relationship between science and religion is an uneasy one, though. The book *Science and Belief*,[4] by the Christian physicist Russell Stannard, carries an endorsement by the biologist Lewis Wolpert who says, "It is a puzzle that scientists can be religious, but Russell Stannard gives an excellent account of his beliefs." So one well-known, intelligent, rational scientist can reject religion, even after reading an "excellent" account of how another such scientist can embrace it.

There is a wide range of opinions on the current state of the relationship. At one extreme is the view that science and religion are directly in conflict; if one is right, the other must be wrong. Fundamentalists on both sides believe this 'conflict' view, but so do casual observers of the media who have had no contact with religion, and have only ever come across the entrenched, confrontational style of debate.

As the Introduction pointed out, analytically inclined people who hold this 'conflict' view may think of religion as a superstitious relic from long ago, having no relevance today. However, polls repeatedly show that a large proportion of people hold religious views of some kind – from about 40 percent up to 90 percent, depending on the questions asked. That weight of numbers doesn't prove that their religious views are correct, but they cannot *all* be dismissed as impressionable, irrational, uncritical and superstitious people. None of the religious scientists named earlier would fit that description, for example.

Some religious people who hold the 'conflict' type of view will deny the validity of good scientific results that seem to contradict the teachings of their religion. They will simply ignore any evidence that supports the correctness of such results.

At the opposite extreme from the 'conflict' view, is the view that science is about the workings of the universe, whilst religion is about matters such as morals, values and relationships; in this view, science and religion are assumed not to overlap at all, so there is no conflict.

I find neither of these views convincing, though the second is much nearer to the truth. Everyday experience indicates that the fields of science and religion do overlap. For example, someone who believes that God answers prayers, must also believe that God acts in the world today in providing those answers. If that is true, then observations of the world after God's actions will presumably be different from what science would have predicted before them.

If, for example, prayers have been said for someone who, according to our best medical science, was terminally ill, and he has recovered, what should we make of it? Was the diagnosis incorrect, was it a coincidence, was it due to something science has not yet discovered, was it a miracle in answer to prayer – and can we ever know?

In addressing questions such as those listed in the Introduction, this book suggests that science and religion are both valid ways of viewing the universe, and that they can complement each other. If you share Wolpert's puzzlement, then there are some explanations here, not only of why the puzzlement arises, but also of how scientists can be religious. What's more, this harmonization is possible without either needing to regard religion as irrational, or needing to deny any well-researched scientific results.

In this chapter, and the next, we begin by looking at some general ideas that will apply to more specific topics later.

## What is the scientific method?

Readers whose education or employment has been mainly in non-scientific areas may not fully appreciate how scientists go about their work. That is going to be important to us, so this section introduces the 'scientific method' of analyzing the universe. It was built upon the early seventeenth century ideas of Francis Bacon and, in my own experience, can be summarized as follows.

It begins when a scientist makes an intriguing observation, or has an idea that awakens her interest in some particular phenomenon. The topic of interest can be almost anything. It might concern the distribution of the galaxies in space, or how to cure a particular disease, or how a couple of meters of DNA is packed into each of the trillions (that's millions of millions) of cells which make up each of us, or how to generate clean energy by nuclear fusion, or how to confirm the existence of some postulated sub-atomic particle of matter, or how to automatically control the flatness of stainless steel in a rolling mill (the irresistibly-interesting subject of my PhD).

The scientist then formulates a potential solution to the problem at hand. She uses a combination of approaches; such as making careful observations; analysis using mathematics, physics, chemistry, molecular biology, or whatever other techniques are necessary; and adapting any relevant work of other scientists. At this stage, the tentative solution is called a hypothesis.

Next, the scientist tries to devise experiments that will confirm her hypothesis. Sometimes these are physical experiments, carried out in a laboratory; or on an item of industrial plant; or even in a multi-billion dollar, purpose-built facility. Sometimes, the experimentation is more theoretical, based on the analysis of mathematical descriptions and computer simulations.

If her hypothesis can pass every test she can devise, the scientist comes to a particularly important aspect of this approach: she publishes her work in sufficient detail that anyone else can repeat it to check her findings. Other scientists may develop alternative experiments, in an effort to submit the new idea to as wide a range of tests as possible.

A new hypothesis will sometimes predict that further specific discoveries ought to be made if it is true, and experiments can then be devised to see whether these predictions are correct. If they are, that's usually an excellent indicator that the scientists are on the right track.

However, no matter how many successful tests are carried out, they only provide increasing confidence that the hypothesis is correct; they don't *prove* it. If even one repeatable, unsuccessful test can be found, it shows that the hypothesis is wrong – the scientists must refine their ideas and try again. A scientific hypothesis can thus be disproved, but it cannot be conclusively proved, so once a new idea has passed every test that can currently be conceived, it attains the status of a 'theory', not a proven fact.

When I first began to think about the relationship between science and religion, I was influenced by a suggestion that the theory of evolution is "only a theory", the implication being that I shouldn't take evolution too seriously as it could easily be wrong. We must return to the question of evolution later but, for now, the previous discussion demonstrates that my teenage view was misguided, being based on an incomplete understanding of the scientific method. It was like saying that the theory of gravitation is only a theory, so we can ignore gravity if we like.

Once a piece of knowledge attains the status of a scientific theory, it is actually the best that we can do at the time. The theory may eventually need updating; but even then we shall not normally have to discard the previous theory altogether. For example, the previous theory may turn out to be a special case in a new, more general, theory.

Let's briefly look at gravitation as an example of how a scientific theory develops. After earlier ideas by Galileo and others, Isaac

Newton published his theory of gravity in 1687. It remained our best theory of gravity for almost 230 years. Then, in 1916, Albert Einstein published his general theory of relativity, which has survived many stringent and ingenious experimental tests.

Even though general relativity has replaced Newton's theory as our most accurate gravitational theory, Newton's theory has not been abandoned. For bodies separated by distances ranging from a millimeter or so, to the largest distances in the universe, it remains a very good approximation to reality, unless gravitational fields are exceptionally strong, or speeds are a significant fraction of the speed of light. It is still taught in schools and colleges, it is good enough to land men on The Moon, and it is much easier to use than Einstein's theory. Physicists are searching for the next gravitational theory, which will apply at sub-atomic distances, where even Einstein's theory breaks down.[5]

Returning to the scientific method, there can be obstacles to its 'pure' application. For example, it is not always clear how data should be interpreted, which can lead to alternative acceptable explanations of the same thing. Over a century after the dawn of quantum theory (one of the more bizarre areas of physics), there are still fundamental differences of opinion as to how to interpret some aspects of it. Also, scientists are only human, so it is not unknown for results to be biased by motives other than purely scientific ones. However, since the public scrutiny of results by other scientists eventually weeds out such aberrations, the method is self-correcting.

Bearing in mind the rigor of the scientific method, imagine that a religious person dismisses a well-researched scientific theory. In response, a scientist explains all the publically available evidence, and the careful series of investigations, which have led to that theory. If the religious person then simply replies, "Well, we have a holy book which says differently, so you must be wrong", you can perhaps appreciate the scientist's resulting frustration with religion.

If someone wants to deny a well-researched theory of modern science, he needs to take into account several things: the rigorous, evidence-based, procedures which went into forming the theory; the very high likelihood that it will not be completely wrong; and the effect that his denial will have on his credibility amongst the scientific community. Unless, of course, he can come up with a scientifically testable alternative explanation; then he will be participating in the science.

It is often said that science is about the 'how' questions of the universe. Accordingly, this book uses 'how' in questions about the mechanisms and processes by which things, including us, have come to be as they are, and by which the universe works today. In contrast, it uses 'why' in questions involving matters such as purposes or intentions, desires, morals, ethics, values and truth.

Those 'why' questions lie outside the scope of impersonal scientific explanation, because they don't exist in a form which can be measured, analyzed, and repeatably tested by experiments. Some argue that such things do exist 'scientifically' in our heads, as specific brain-states; but science still doesn't help here. If a scientist measures some particular state of your brain, and wants to correlate it with what you are thinking, she can only discover what you are thinking by asking you. 'Personal explanations', which will be defined shortly, are the appropriate ones for matters such as these.

## Faith and science

Religion is about the 'why' kind of question, often linked to God's intentions for the universe and its inhabitants. Religions also concern themselves with relationships between people and, in most religions, between people and a god.

Actually, I wouldn't like to be described as 'the religious type', because of the negative connotations. These include the common notions that 'the religious type' of person might push his views onto unwilling listeners; he might insist upon backing up what he says by quoting from a holy book in which his listeners have no reason to believe; he might uncritically accept superstitious mumbo-jumbo, in the face of good scientific evidence to the contrary; he may be hypocritical; he might consider himself better than other people; he may even be generally creepy!

If religious people are to create a positive impression, none of that should be true. Nevertheless, it is the kind of stereotype that some atheists project onto religious people. Sadly, there is no smoke without fire in some cases.

In the interests of avoiding specialist theological language, we shall continue to use the word 'religious'. However, please read it without any negative stereotypes in mind because, whether we consider ourselves religious or not, we do all live by faith in something.

For example, sharp-brained philosophers have been arguing for millennia about whether God exists, so it does seem unlikely that there is to be a final, watertight, logical proof of God's existence. If such a proof were to emerge though, we would all eventually become believers. What is less widely recognized is that the converse is also true; there is unlikely to be a watertight, logical proof that God does not exist. If such a proof were to emerge, we would all become atheists. There is more about proof in the next chapter.

So, whether we are believers in a god, or believers that there is no god, we each hold those beliefs by faith, because we cannot logically prove them to be true, and some rational people hold the opposite view to ours. Each of us therefore has to consider the evidence for ourselves, and come to the conclusion that we consider to be the best explanation of the way things seem to be – but getting it right may be gravely important.

We should also be respectful of those who hold the opposite view to ours, since that is also a rational possibility. It doesn't always work like that though; there are those, on either side, who will resort to shouting loudly, literally or in print, when they reach the end of reasoned argument. I respect people of many faiths, including atheism, and hope that they will find this book interesting, since much of the material applies to the kind of relationship any god might have with a universe.

It is also worth recognizing that science itself is undertaken by faith. As one example, there are some physical quantities, such as the speed of light, which are called universal constants, or fundamental constants of nature. Others include the gravitational constant, the electrical charge on an electron and Planck's constant. It doesn't matter if you don't know what these constants are used for; the point is that there are several of them, and perhaps the most interesting thing about them is that scientists haven't a clue as to why they have the particular values they do.

Taking the speed of light as an example, we can perform experiments that tell us that it is about 300,000 kilometers per second (or 186,000 miles per second). We know *how* we obtain that value, but nobody knows *why* it is that value, rather than some other. Scientists would love to have a 'theory of everything' that would allow them to *derive* the value from the theory, but we don't; instead, we can only *measure* the value, which seems to be built into the universe. The same applies to the other universal constants.

Having measured the values of these constants, scientists then incorporate them into the 'laws of science' which they have discovered (or 'laws of nature', if you prefer), and simply assume that those laws apply everywhere in the universe. That's why the constants are called "universal", but actually there is no scientific justification for assuming that the values themselves, or the laws in which they are used, can be applied at all times and in all places. When, for example, we use Einstein's theories to analyze and predict the behavior of galaxies far, far away, or terrestrial nuclear physics to analyze how stars work, we just have faith that it works.

This begins to suggest that science and religion are not as far apart as many people think, since both are underpinned by faith to some extent. Someone might immediately object that the faith of scientists is justified because the resulting theories make sense and seem to correspond with reality, whereas religious faith seems, relatively speaking, baseless. However, that is not the case.

Faith isn't, "believing what you know ain't so",[6] or having to, "believe six impossible things before breakfast";[7] the faith of scientists, as described above, makes that clear. Religious faith is not so different. When I became a Christian, I still had some important doubts about the relationship between science and religion. My faith arose from the dawning realization that I needed God in my life, and it was based on the belief that he would come into my life and do the things he promises to do in the Bible – in terms of giving peace and a deeper purpose to life, for example. I also had faith that any remaining significant gaps, or misunderstandings, in my knowledge would get sorted out in due course. Such faith has been repaid over the years, and my faith, and that of many of my friends, has also been demonstrated to work in the real world; even when 'the real world' is the world of science.

There are other responses to a claim that religious faith is baseless. One is that theologians actually go about their task of investigating the nature of God, in a similar way to the methods used by scientists in investigating the nature of the universe. Clearly, no physical experimentation is possible in theology, but theologians do think carefully about the ideas they develop, they do publish them so that other theologians can examine them and add their own arguments for or against, and the ideas are gradually refined as a result. That is quite similar to what scientists have to do when developing theoretical ideas for which no physical tests exist.

Another relevant point is that it is almost impossible for a non-religious person to appreciate the workings of a religious person's faith. A living faith can be so central to someone in her day-to-day life that it colors everything she thinks and does. Its effects are likely to be definite and can often be observed by others. It's not unlike having a baby – even after you have read all the books and are sure that you understand what it is going to be like, it can still turn your life upside down in unexpected ways when it actually happens to you.

Despite discussions in books like this one, such a living faith is rarely acquired on the basis of intellectual argument alone. It requires an encounter with God. It is much more than attending a mosque on Friday, a synagogue on Saturday, or a church on Sunday. If you have such a faith, you will already understand this. If you don't, perhaps an illustration might help.

Most scientists currently accept that sub-atomic entities such as electrons, quarks and gluons, are the fundamental building blocks of all matter. These are normally bound up inside atoms and, even when they are not (for example, just after a high-energy collision in a particle accelerator experiment) they are vanishingly small. It is therefore impossible directly to observe them. In that sense, even though they are thought to be the basis of all matter, there is no final proof that they exist. Nevertheless, scientists feel justified in having faith in the existence of sub-atomic particles because of the effects they seem to have on larger particles. Also, by assuming that they do exist, and deriving expectations of the behavior of matter from that assumption, they can explain both the results of their experiments, and the existence and properties of everyday matter as we observe it.

In a similar way, the suggestions of religious ideas, and the reality of someone else's religious faith, cannot be logically proved. However, if an acceptance that a believer has had an experience of God is the simplest explanation for his changed behavior, then that might well be taken as confirmation that it is likely to be true – God exists and has changed his life.

As to the title of this book, "a working faith" implies a living faith in God, which also works in the real world, in the sense that it also accords with our best scientific explanations of how the universe came to be, and how it operates. My Christian faith achieves that for me, and some of the reasons for that will emerge later.

## Different types of explanation

You may remember the simple example about the boiling kettle, in the Introduction. Here's a slightly more thorough one, still using an uncontroversial question to which there is more than one kind of answer: "Why is the temperature in the oven 200°C?" Here's an abbreviated scientific answer, assuming an electric oven.

"When the oven was first switched on, an electric current began to pass through the resistive heating element inside the oven. The element therefore got hot, and its heat energy passed into the interior of the oven, causing the oven's temperature to rise; all these things can be calculated, and predicted. The oven has a thermostat which has been set to 200°C. When the temperature in the oven slightly exceeded 200°C for the first time, the thermostat disconnected the electrical supply from the element. The oven then began to cool as its heat energy began leaking away into the room. Once its temperature was slightly lower than 200°C, the thermostat reconnected the supply, so that the oven heated up again. That on-off switching cycle of the electrical heating element is now repeating, and will continue to do so for as long as the oven is switched on, resulting in an average temperature of 200°C in the oven."

A completely non-technical answer to the question, "Why is the oven at 200°C?" is, "because I am about to cook a roast dinner."

Nobody is upset by the differences between these two answers (though they might be upset by my roast dinner), and nobody would deny that both answers are valid. Either can be used, depending on the circumstances: is the question part of a science examination paper, or is it addressed to a friend in the kitchen?

The scientific answer is about the 'how' of the situation, in the sense of, "what are the *processes* and *mechanisms* which have led to the temperature being 200°C?" The non-technical answer is about the 'why' – "what is the *purpose* of the temperature being 200°C?" The purpose is completely irrelevant to the purely scientific answer, whilst the processes and mechanisms by which the oven operates are completely irrelevant to the purely non-technical answer. Nevertheless, both descriptions are required for a complete explanation of the situation.

In the example above, the two explanations were entirely complementary, but alternative explanations can sometimes seem to be in conflict. As an example, there are at least two well-known descriptions of the creation of the universe.

There is a well-justified description, which is accepted by the majority of scientists. We shall return to this later but, for now, a sketchy description will suffice. About 13.7 billion years ago (13,700 million years ago),[8] in a 'big bang', unimaginably hot matter, space and time all came into existence. As the very early universe cooled, much of the matter rapidly became arranged into vast quantities of hydrogen and helium, which then clumped together under the influence of gravity, to form stars.

Stars are nuclear furnaces, in which chemical elements heavier than hydrogen are formed. At the ends of their lives, some of the first stars exploded (this is normal for a certain type of star), creating even heavier elements and releasing them into space.

Again under the influence of gravity, the resulting clouds of matter re-aggregated into new stars, but with an important difference: elements such as iron, nickel, carbon, oxygen, silicon, aluminum and calcium, necessary for forming rocks, were now present. Some of those new stars could therefore have solar systems, including rocky planets. One such solar system is ours, in which Earth formed about 4.5 billion years ago.

As Earth cooled, an atmosphere formed, followed by complex chemicals that eventually gave rise to life. That first life gradually evolved, leading to the appearance of modern humans about 200,000 years ago. Your brain, with its 85 billion interconnected neurons, which has evolved sufficiently to allow you to appreciate this, is believed to be the most complex entity in the universe.

Apart from an extremely tiny fraction of the first second after the big bang, scientists have developed detailed descriptions of most (though not yet all) of the processes involved in that sequence of events. The results are widely documented, and are in good agreement with observations and experiments. This is currently our best scientific explanation for the origin of the types of matter that make up the universe; and the structures, from galaxies to people, into which that matter has become arranged.

On the other hand, there are creation stories from several ancient cultures and religions. The Judeo-Christian version, if understood literally from the book of Genesis in English translations of the Bible, suggests that creation happened over a period of six days. It began with God saying, "Let there be light" on the first day, and proceeded via the creation of the various components of the universe and Earth's biosphere, to the direct creation of people like us, on the sixth. We shall look briefly at that biblical sequence of events later, and compare it with the scientific description – the result is interesting.

In the 17th century, an Irish Archbishop, James Ussher, used various biblical lists of family histories, and similar records, to date the act of creation, as reported in the Bible, at 4004 BC. Others came up with similar dates, some claiming to have derived a specific day and time.

The scientific story and the biblical story both claim to explain the creation of the same universe; therefore they should not be in conflict in any areas where they overlap. If they were complementary, as in the case of the hot oven, then all would be well. However, there is a conflict between the two explanations as presented above, so at least one of them must be wrong.

Returning to the example of the hot oven, the reason that there is no conflict between the two explanations is due to the fact that the second, "Because I am about to cook a roast dinner", is entirely non-scientific. Such explanations are sometimes called *personal explanations*, in contrast to the *impersonal* explanations of science.

Scientific explanations deliberately exclude anything personal, so that experiments and analyses don't depend on some special characteristic, or memory, of the person carrying them out. The experiments must be able to be repeated by anyone with the correct scientific training and equipment. That's why, when you were writing up science experiments at school, you were probably taught not to write, "I then did so-and-so...", but rather to write, "Such-and-such was then done..."; it removed you from the process and made it impersonal, and hence able to be repeated by anyone else.

What about the biblical explanation of the creation story? For me, the key is to recognize that the Christian Bible is not a single book; the protestant version is a library of 66 books, of several different kinds (genres), written by about 40 different authors, over a period of about 1,500 years. It contains books of poetry, history, teaching material, prophecy, wisdom literature (such as proverbs), allegory (stories designed to point to a hidden meaning), letters, and so on. A fundamental aspect of understanding any part of the Bible is therefore to work out what type of book is being read at the time.

In a normal library, if you picked up a book entitled *The Kings of Scotland*, you would expect it to contain an accurate history of Scottish kings. However, if you picked up a book entitled *Macbeth*, you would discover that it was a Shakespeare play about Scottish kings. The play does contain information about the deeds of Scottish kings, but it would never occur to you to interpret it literally, as history.

In the library of books that constitutes the Bible, one type of book that you will not find is a science text. The Bible was written in an age long before modern science; in fact, some scholars suggest that parts of the book of Genesis are 3,400 years old, which places them in the Bronze Age.[9]

If Genesis isn't a science text, what is it? It might be described as poetic literature with a purpose or, as in the words of the astrophysicist and theologian David Wilkinson, Genesis is not "About the 'how' of creation, nor even primarily about the 'why' of creation. Rather, it is a passage about the 'who' of creation, and is an overture [to the whole Bible] which introduces us to the Creator God."[10] All this confirms that those early parts of Genesis are not to be interpreted as literal scientific explanations.

Interestingly, in addition to some religious people, many atheists like to assume a literal interpretation of the early part of Genesis. The religious people perhaps do so because they think they ought to, even though it causes problems when compared with modern science. Some atheists do so simply through ignorance of the structure of the Bible. However, others do so deliberately, because they can then more easily make a cheap point about the Bible's assumed unreliability. In doing so, both the religious people and the atheists are effectively reading Genesis as though it was intended to be a science text, which it was not.

What we might make of the actual wording in Genesis, to resolve the apparent conflict with the scientific explanation, is something to which we shall return later. For now, the view in this book is that the big bang was God's chosen method of creation; and that evolution, however it is generally understood by modern science, is God's chosen method of allowing life to develop on Earth. Genesis is a book written in ancient times, which covers that ground in a way meaningful to those bronze-age people and, more importantly for us, fulfills the purpose suggested by the earlier quotation from Wilkinson.

In general, since personal explanations are complementary to scientific ones, thinking of religious descriptions in terms of personal explanations can go a long way towards reducing potential conflict where science and religion overlap.

# Chapter 2  Science and Religion –
## Some Wider Issues

Whilst Chapter One looked at some of the basic differences and similarities between science and religion, this chapter looks at some more subtle general matters relevant to the remainder of the book.

## What is the problem with proof?

Given the choice between a single definitive answer to a question, and a compromise between two or more competing answers, I prefer the situation in which there is only one right answer. This is probably due to whatever personality traits led to my analytical, scientific background, but I am far from alone in wishing for irrefutable answers to questions.

Unfortunately though, demonstrating that there is only one correct answer to a problem requires proof and, as we have already seen, that may be hard to obtain.

When reading books which cover similar areas to this one, I have often wished that the authors would explain at least a little about what brought them to the views they hold. A few paragraphs of autobiography follow (any more would be too tedious), which indicate why some thinking about proof was necessary for me.

When I was extremely young, I was even more interested than most small boys in cars, motorcycles, cranes, diggers, planes, boats and so on. That hasn't changed – on my most recent birthday I received several cards, an acceptable proportion of which still carried pictures of vehicles of one sort or another. I was 61 (clearly a very young 61 though).

Similarly, I have always been fascinated by how things – any things – work. I was cleaning and re-packing the bearings on my bicycles as soon as I reached an age at which it was physically possible to do so. I made a bit of money in my teenage years by mending radios and televisions, and by building domestic audio systems, as well as amplifiers and light shows for bands and discos.

The writing was on the wall. During my schooldays, whenever a choice between subjects had to be made, it was inevitable that I would choose the more technical option. It was equally inevitable that, when it came to choosing a degree course, it would be a technical one (control systems engineering, in fact). I have spent my working life in control system analysis and design, and I still teach the occasional university course on control systems, even though I have officially retired.

Like the science, my faith has to make sense in the real world as far as is possible, so it must not contradict any good science. I was attending a Christian church before I was even born, and was taken there every Sunday once I had emerged into the world. Every year, I won prizes for regular attendance. I still have a couple of books, chosen as such prizes when I was eight and ten years old; they are both of a scientific nature.

I continued to attend church every Sunday (sometimes three times on a Sunday, in those days), but under protest once I reached my teenage years. I had a good father, and I am grateful to him for many things. One of those things, though I didn't appreciate it at the time, was that he could be quite strict. In the interests of family harmony, it often seemed better not to make a fuss about attending church, and just to continue to do so. The down-side was that I was sometimes – how shall I put this – not a very helpful person to have in the Sunday School classes; I was occasionally ejected for being disruptive.

When I reached my mid-to-late teenage years, several of my church friends were taking the definite step of 'becoming a Christian'. I did not. When I was about 17, I was sitting in a church service one Sunday evening. The preacher was delivering an evangelical sermon, explaining to us the benefits of asking God into our lives. There was nothing unusual about that but, on this particular occasion, I remember thinking, "This is all very well, but firstly you need to prove to me that God exists; I'm not yet convinced."

When I was much younger, I never doubted that God existed; it went with the territory of going to church every Sunday, and absorbing what the Sunday school teachers, and my parents, told me. As I grew older, I became much less sure about God's existence, especially in the light of my rapidly increasing scientific knowledge of the universe. It seemed sensible to me that the first step was to be sure that God really exists, before I could be expected to put my trust in him. Sadly, despite my almost 100 percent church attendance record, nothing had totally convinced me that God exists; everything else connected with Christianity therefore had a rather theoretical feel.

The reason I recall this occasion is that it led to a decision to read more books, which eventually led to the resolution of such difficulties. With the benefit of hindsight, I would say that God was guiding me, in a way that I didn't realize at the time. I also think it is an example of how God can begin to work in people's lives if they let him.

I was open to God's working because I was serious about discovering something to do with his existence, and hence about the effects that he was having in the lives of some of my friends. If I had taken the stance of rejecting him, or just ignoring him completely, this guidance would probably not have been forthcoming. As it is, the fact that I did something as straightforward as following up an impulse to do some more reading, directly contributed to my becoming a Christian.

In my reading, I soon discovered that nobody would ever be able to prove conclusively that God exists. In its technical sense, to prove something is to demonstrate that it could not possibly be any other way; if an idea is proved in that sense, no alternative can exist. Unfortunately, there is hardly anything outside of mathematics and formal logic that can strictly be proved. What's more, even in those fields, proofs can only succeed if everyone agrees to certain axioms – non-provable statements that just have to be accepted as a basis from which to begin.

With that definition of proof in mind, it is unlikely that a strict proof will exist for anything of interest to us in this book. There will probably always be at least one alternative argument, with which at least some reasonable people will agree. The existence of such alternative rational explanations, even if they are very unlikely ones, means that the suggested 'proof' is not a strict proof after all, because things could be otherwise.

As a specific example, let's propose that Earth is about 4.5 billion years old, and that dinosaurs once lived on it. Most educated people have some scientific knowledge, even if it is only from school, or from popular-science in books or television programs. Anyone who has acquired that sort of popular-science background might well have become convinced that the study of geology, the fossil record, and the dating of rocks by measuring the products of radioactive decay do, indeed, prove that Earth is about 4.5 billion years old, and that dinosaurs once lived on it.

Many of us are convinced that this is the best explanation of the evidence. Nevertheless, it doesn't actually *prove* anything, because there are alternative explanations that cannot be disproved. For example, science cannot disprove the possibility that Earth could be much younger than it appears. However unlikely you (and I) might think it to be, Earth could somehow have been formed relatively recently, perhaps by an all-powerful God, with something like the presently-visible geology already in place, with fossils of dinosaurs already present in the rocks; and with rocks containing proportions of radioactive uranium, thorium and potassium which suggest that they are hundreds of millions of years old.

We each have to weigh the evidence, and come to what we consider to be the best explanation of the facts. Anyone who wants to believe the second suggestion above is on safe ground, in the sense that nobody can strictly prove that it is wrong.

The proposition that Earth is about 4.5 billion years old, and that dinosaurs once lived on it, is therefore capable of being either accepted, or rejected; there is no absolutely certain proof either way.

However, the scientific evidence that Earth is very old, and that dinosaurs lived on it, seems overwhelming. Also, no god worth worshipping would be so capricious as to fill the rocks with geology and fossils calculated to mislead generations of well-meaning geologists and paleontologists; some of whom will also be religious. Therefore, I accept the 'old Earth' proposition simply because it seems, to me, the best explanation of the facts. In later chapters, we shall look more closely at the evidence that Earth is very old.

Here's a more everyday example. Every evening, on my local television station, the weather forecaster says, "The Sun will rise tomorrow at... ", followed by the appropriate time. In fact, the forecaster isn't strictly correct in saying that. Nobody can prove that The Sun will rise tomorrow at all, though there is probably no reasonable person on the planet who would bet against it, as it would take some truly cataclysmic event to prevent it. The point is though, that we cannot actually prove that no such event will occur, however unlikely it might be. We all, including the scientifically trained weather forecaster, just have faith that The Sun will rise tomorrow, following the usual laws of nature.

Proof, in this sense, is therefore an extremely strong requirement. It is even difficult to obtain in cases, which, at first sight, may seem blindingly obvious. For example, even on a blindingly sunny day, we cannot actually prove that The Sun is shining at any particular instant. Pointing at it and saying, "Look – there it is!" is not good enough, because it takes the light from The Sun about 500 seconds to travel the 150 million kilometers (93 million miles) from The Sun to Earth.

Therefore, although it is highly improbable, if some catastrophe has stopped The Sun from shining at any time during the last eight minutes or so, we will not yet know about it. Until that transit time expires, we will continue to see the sunlight that has been on its way to us since before the catastrophe occurred.

Examples like these reinforce the view that even the most atheistic, and the most rational, of us therefore live our lives by faith, to some extent.

Of course, if you think that the existence of God is so unlikely that it might just as well be the case that he has been proved not to exist, then you might take quite a lot of convincing that he does exist. Nevertheless, it cannot be proved that God doesn't exist, and a huge number of reasonable people think that he does.

Many people have put forward 'proofs' for God down the years, one of whom was Anselm. He lived in the eleventh and twelfth centuries and, amongst other things, he became the Archbishop of Canterbury. He defined God as, "That than which nothing greater can be conceived", a definition that still stands today. From his definition, he then claimed to develop a proof of God's existence.

Although Anselm's 'proof' doesn't stand up to modern scrutiny, the philosopher Alvin Plantinga has carefully analyzed it, and from it he does claim to have developed a strict proof that belief in God is at least a reasonable belief to hold.[11] If that is true, then nobody can now deny that belief in God is at least a rationally acceptable viewpoint; we religious believers are not simply deluded or deranged.

## Nothing buttery

This section looks further into the question of whether scientific explanations alone can ever be sufficient.

The brain scientist Donald MacKay coined the phrase "nothing buttery".[12] It is a shorthand description of a particular form of what philosophers call 'reductionism'. Put simply, it is the idea that once you have explained the individual parts that make up something, you have explained the thing itself.

Giving some examples of the impression that had been created by anti-religious writers in the middle of the twentieth century, MacKay wrote, "Christians believed that the world was created by God; Science (with a capital S) showed that 'really' it was 'nothing but' a fortuitous concourse of atoms. Christians thanked God for sending rain and daily bread; Science explained the agricultural cycle as 'nothing but' the workings of an intricate physical mechanism. Christians believed that they had direct evidence of God's dealings with them in their daily experience; Science claimed that soon, if not now, this could be reduced to 'nothing but' the running of their psychological machinery." MacKay went on to demonstrate the fallacy of these claims of 'Science'.

Here's a personal example. Music is one of the few things that can bring a tear to my eye. No doubt this is partly because I come from a musical family, and have played a number of instruments in various bands and orchestras, and sung in various bands and choirs, for more than fifty years. Feeling the moving quality of music is not unique to musicians though; people of all kinds find it moving, in a way that language generally is not.

Musical instruments produce their sounds when the musicians cause vibrations in various mechanical elements – strings, cymbals, drum skins, reeds or columns of air in the case of wind instruments, and so on. These vibrations pass through the air as sound waves, mixing with the vibrations from the other instruments. When you listen to a symphony orchestra or a rock band, it is these vibrations in the air that reach your ears, to be interpreted by your brain as a complex set of sounds.

The sound waves reaching your ears can be analyzed, and reduced to their basic components – a set of pure tones (sinusoidal waves, in scientific terminology). A bank of electronic oscillators can then be constructed to duplicate the shapes of each of those pure tones, and their relationships with each other, and then mix them together to recreate the original sound. Or a computer can be programmed to do the same thing, which is easier these days. Either way, in scientific terms this results in synthesizing the sound from the amplitudes (sizes), frequencies (pitches) and phase shifts (differences in timing) of the set of pure tones that constitutes it.

It is important to note that this is not simply a digitized *recording* of the sound, such as would be found in an MP3 file, or on an audio CD. Rather, it is a *reconstruction* of the sound from the set of many, individually generated, pure sound waves, which are its most fundamental components. Nevertheless, in principle this reconstruction can be done so well that you would be hard-pressed to tell the difference between the synthesized version and the original live sound.

The point of all this is that a reductionist person may now feel justified in saying that the sound is 'nothing but' a collection of waveforms, having carefully-specified characteristics.

In terms only of the physics, and the engineering of the synthesized sounds, that description might be acceptable. However, although it might be an accurate scientific description of the sounds, so complete that it enables them to be regenerated, accurately, anywhere in the world, *it spectacularly misses the point.*

In the above description of the development of the synthesized version of the sounds, it was not necessary to mention that the sounds were a piece of music in a concert venue; that was completely irrelevant to the process. If you doubt it, re-read the four preceding paragraphs, starting from "The sound waves reaching your ears...".

In fact, it is the personal explanation which gives the whole reason for the events in this case: a composer had the desire to compose a piece of music, a concert promoter formed the intention of presenting that piece of music to the public, and people had the notion that going to a concert would be a worthwhile way of enjoying themselves for an evening.

Had it not been for the intention in the mind of the composer, the scientific analysis of those particular sounds would have been impossible, as they would never have existed. The very existence of the scientific explanation is entirely dependent on the personal explanation.

The parallel in the discussion of science and religion is that it may be very unwise to claim that the universe is 'nothing but' the out-workings of the laws of nature, starting from a certain set of initial conditions, when science doesn't know where those laws of nature, or the initial conditions, came from.

Many rational people do claim to know though – they claim that the laws of nature, and the initial conditions of the universe, arose in the Mind of God. If that is correct, we can only do our science at all because of the intention in the Mind of God to create a universe, in the same way that we can only analyze the sounds in the concert hall because of the intention in the mind of the composer to create a piece of music.

Nobody can conclusively prove whether that idea is right or wrong, but it seems to be at least rational; it cannot simply be dismissed as nonsense.

The idea of God as the Mind behind the universe is, like many of the ideas in this book, very old. In ancient Greece, Socrates and his pupil Plato believed that 'Mind' is ultimately responsible for the existence of matter, and for keeping it in existence. Plato's pupil Aristotle thought that the universe is governed by some kind of purposeful design. He devised a system of 'motions' and 'causes' for everything, and equated the first cause of everything, the 'unmoved mover', with God.

In the thirteenth century, the eminent scholar Thomas Aquinas came up with his famous line, "The existence of God can be proved in five ways", and presented his five 'proofs'.[13] Again, these are not strict 'proofs' by modern standards, but they do form the basis of some modern arguments. For example, the philosopher and theologian Keith Ward points out that that we need to consider what kinds of explanations there could be for the universe. In particular, he says that, "Serious consideration of the arguments of the Five Ways requires acceptance that personal explanation is a proper and irreducible form of explanation, and that the existence of an ultimate mind as the source of all reality is a coherent and plausible notion."[14]

Ward goes on to say, "The Five Ways can be seen as articulations of the idea of ultimate mind as the final personal explanation of the universe. If that idea is dismissed at the outset, the proofs cannot succeed. But if the idea is accepted as a real possibility, then the proofs both provide more detailed specifications of the idea, and provide good reasons for accepting that the idea corresponds to reality – that there is a God."

## Where is the god of the gaps?

In earlier ages most people were inclined to believe in God, since God seemed to be the only possible explanation for things they observed on Earth and in the skies. Effectively, they were saying, "Here is something we cannot explain, so God must have done it." As the centuries have passed, science has closed up many of those gaps into which we used to put God. The "god of the gaps" is now a phrase often used, in a dismissive way, to describe a god who is forced to retreat under the onslaught of science, and will soon have no gaps left in which to hide.

Modern science (including engineering) is certainly very impressive. It has resulted in all our modern buildings, roads, transport systems and vehicles; hospitals and medical procedures, equipment and pharmaceuticals; production and distribution of processed food and drink; space travel and satellites; computing systems, communication systems, entertainment systems and domestic appliances; the production and distribution of electricity, gas, mains water, petrol, diesel and fuel oil; and also of the materials we use, such as glass, plastics, other chemicals, textiles, paper, processed wood and refined metals. This list could go on for pages.

As a result of this all-pervading success of science, less-scientific people can have a tendency to think that scientists, as a body, know everything, and that they have proved, beyond question, the validity of every piece of science mentioned in the media. Actually, no reputable scientist would agree. However, many would still say that we no longer need to invoke God to explain the moment of creation, because it was the big bang; and we no longer need to invoke God to explain the origin of human beings, because it was evolution. Those are just two significant gaps in which we used to put God, which now seem to have been closed by science.

Are there still gaps in our knowledge that God might fill? There are certainly plenty of things that we still don't understand; we have already mentioned some in connection with creation. Also, although there is a chapter on evolution later, it's worth mentioning here that we don't have much of a clue as to how the first life could have arisen from non-living chemicals. Similarly, we still seem to have only a very limited understanding of consciousness, especially self-consciousness.

However, as long ago as the beginning of the fifth century, Augustine of Hippo (St. Augustine) said, "In Holy Scripture [there are] passages which can be interpreted in very different ways without prejudice to the faith we have received."[15] He went on to say that we should not pin our faith so firmly to one particular interpretation of scripture, that advances in discovering further truths leave us stranded. So it seems that, even from the early days of Christianity, we have known that biblical passages can be open to different, yet perfectly valid, interpretations, and also that 'science' will tend to advance, and close up gaps in which we might have placed God (in Augustine's day the 'science' would have been the philosophy of Aristotle, rather than science as we now know it, but the point remains valid).

Today, it is even more the case that it would be unwise to look at gaps in our knowledge, and say, "We don't understand that, so it must be due to God." The history of scientific progress over the last few hundred years suggests that modern science is really good at closing such gaps.

Instead, religious people can relax in the benefits which their religion brings to their everyday lives, and in the personal explanations, which are complementary to the scientific ones – for example, that the universe is fulfilling the purposes of God, and that he upholds it from day to day and continues to seek relationships with us.

None of those statements is testable by the scientific method, so it does seem that it will always be possible for religious people to be able to make that kind of claim, no matter what extra discoveries science might make about the origin of the universe, or of humankind. It will always be a rational option to claim that the universe was God's idea, and that science is "Thinking God's thoughts after him", as Kepler said so long ago. It could be that, after all, the most fundamental aspect of the universe is not the science, but God's purposes.

Purely as a matter of interest, and not fundamental to the arguments of this book, it is unlikely that science will ever complete its "Theory of Everything". The details are too technical to describe here, but the comment arises from work of the mathematician Kurt Gödel, who published two "incompleteness theorems" in the early 1930s. Put simplistically, these prove (yes, strictly) that any system that uses ordinary arithmetic will contain statements that cannot be proved. As the mathematician John Lennox points out, since any potential "Theory of Everything" must use arithmetic, it can therefore never be complete, in the sense of being a theory in which everything can be proved.[16]

## Surely it's not all intellectual?

Despite the fact that this book addresses some difficult questions, interesting and intellectually satisfying answers to such questions are not the be-all and end-all of the matter.

Firstly, taking the thorny question of suffering as one example, nobody can deny that there is a great deal of pain and suffering in the world, and that this is generally agreed to be a bad thing. It has been confirmed by surveys, and by the direct experiences of religious people whilst talking to non-believers, that this is the greatest single stumbling-block which prevents people from accepting that there is an all-loving, all-powerful God, who cares about them more deeply than any human ever could.

There are rational responses to the problems of suffering, some of which will be mentioned later, but they are likely to be of no help to someone who is actually suffering. For such a person, there may be a more appropriate time for the rational explanation (ideally before the suffering began) but, in the acute stages of suffering, a much more personal and humane response is required. Listening, sympathy, and just 'being there', will usually turn out to be much more useful than reasoning.

Even after the intellectual arguments which attempt to 'explain' the existence of suffering have been made, most of us will still need to pause and take a deep breath, or even shed a tear, at some of the things which happen in the world. Later, we shall see that God might 'shed a tear' with us.

Secondly, not many people are ultimately argued into belief in God. Most of my Christian friends and acquaintances would say that they became Christians after some kind of encounter with God, rather than as a direct result of persuasion by rational argument.

Thirdly, it cannot be the case that one needs a PhD, or an IQ of 150, in order to be able to follow a religion. Assuming that God is loving and fair, an appropriate relationship with him must be available to everyone, whatever their intellectual capacity.

However, although rational argument may not, of itself, finally persuade many people, there are those who genuinely need answers to at least some of their intellectual questions, before they are able seriously to consider the claims of religion. Of course, people with closed minds can simply keep on dreaming up difficult questions indefinitely. Rather, I am thinking of people who are open to changing their minds, so long as there is a sufficient weight of evidence suggesting that it is appropriate to do so. I certainly needed answers to at least some of my intellectual questions before I felt able to consider taking the step of becoming a Christian.

In my late teenage years, my own doubts about Christianity were fairly standard ones, such as a requirement for proof of the existence of God, and the apparent conflict between the first chapters of the Bible and my scientific knowledge of creation and evolution at the time.

Some of my religious friends though, generally those having less-scientific backgrounds, have only limited interest in such questions. They are (mostly) well-educated, intelligent people, but they are happy to accept the beliefs of their religion because it works, and they soon become bored by the types of discussion I might enjoy. However, even for those people, since the differences between science and religion are a talking point in the popular media at present, an indication of some responses to some of the awkward questions might be useful.

In fact, despite the earlier comments about my rational background and scientific outlook, I took the step of becoming a Christian well before I had satisfactory answers to all my questions. That reinforces the point that there is more to this than discovering interesting lines of argument. In particular, it indicates that God does act in people's lives at a deeper level than the purely intellectual.

Ironically, the book that probably did most to help me to take the final step of becoming a Christian was David Watson's book *My God is Real*.[17] I say 'ironically', because this was a very straightforward book, entirely about the human condition, and containing nothing about science. People do sometimes say that God has a sense of humor – excellent!

I only needed to make a limited amount of progress in resolving my intellectual questions, in order to be able to take the step of committing my life to Christ. The most important thing did, indeed, turn out to be the encounter with God; the remaining intellectual questions could wait until later.

We are all different though, and God deals with us accordingly. Although it was necessary for me to have spent *some* time resolving a *few* of the intellectual aspects, it turned out that I didn't have to go anything like as far along that road as I had expected; God was coming the other way, faster than I was travelling, and he met me long before I would have thought that I was ready.

He does seem to do this sometimes – one night, one of my friends went to bed as a worldly atheist; she wasn't consciously searching for God in any way whatsoever. Nevertheless, she woke up in the middle of the night, crying tears of joy, knowing that she had met God, and that she needed to go and find a church! Though she did not know it at the time, she later discovered that whilst she was baby-sitting for a neighbor, the neighbor and a group of that neighbor's Christian friends had been praying for her. She has now been a fine Christian for decades.

## Moving on

Based on the general background provided by these first two chapters, the rest of the book looks in more detail at the interesting questions listed in the Introduction. To begin that process, the next four chapters introduce a few of the wonders of the universe, both very large and very small. As a result, you will find more scientific detail in those chapters than is usual in introductory books on the relationship between science and religion. There are at least four good reasons for this.

Firstly, it is included simply to remind us of some of the wonders of creation, which can fill anyone, whatever their world-view might be, with feelings of awe and wonder. For many people though, this can also reinforce the idea that there is more to the universe than purely rational, scientific explanation. When they look at the night sky, or stand on the summit of a mountain and admire the view, they may appreciate the beauty of the mathematics, physics, geology and biology that underlie the scientific explanations for what they are seeing. However, that seems a completely inadequate explanation for what they actually experience. As an aside, even a dyed-in-the-wool, hard-nosed scientist, who might be satisfied with the purely scientific descriptions of those experiences, can't explain why there actually is that beauty in the underlying mathematics and physics.

Secondly, the scientific detail is included to indicate some of the evidence suggesting that the science presented in the next four chapters actually corresponds to reality, and therefore cannot be denied without good reason. The aim is always to show how the scientific and religious explanations of the universe can complement each other.

Thirdly, it covers several questions that I am asked after giving talks – when there is never enough time to go into the amount of detail included here.

Fourthly, it covers some of the evidence, provided by science itself, that there are limits to our present scientific knowledge, limits to the extent to which science will ever be able to predict all the workings of the universe, and limits to the extent to which science can displace the notion that there is a need for a Creator.

Although the next four chapters do concentrate on the science, they are all relevant to the overlap between science and religion, and they do contain comments on that relationship. If you find that a particular section is getting a bit too technical for your liking, feel free to skim-read to the next section, skipping the technical details, but do be sure to pick out the comments about how it all relates to God. If you do that, you may miss some of the evidence, but you'll still cover the ideas.

Setting aside the science for a moment, it remains the case that if one person believes that God exists, while another believes that he doesn't, only one of them is correct. During the rest of the book I shall therefore also explain a little more about how I, as a well-qualified, rational (or so I've been told), industrial research scientist and university engineering lecturer, also find it entirely sensible to believe in a God whose existence I cannot logically prove. As part of that, I shall also be explaining how I am able to hold my faith without the need to deny any well-researched findings of modern science.

# Chapter 3   Uncertainty and Unpredictability

Recall, from the previous chapter, the 'god of the gaps', whom we have (unwisely) tended to invoke to fill the gaps in our scientific knowledge. We have seen how the advances of science tend to oust God from such 'gaps', by explaining them away. Interestingly though, later discoveries can occasionally open a gap up again – or reveal a different one. It is not the case that the advances of science only ever close such gaps.

It remains unwise to invoke God as an explanation for any such new gap in our knowledge, but it is, nevertheless, interesting when a gap reappears after having been considered closed. In the discussion between science and religion, the emerging 'gap' described in this chapter seems particularly interesting, for reasons which will become clear later.

## Does the universe run like clockwork?

Over the last three hundred years or so, there have often been suggestions that the universe just ticks along like clockwork, following laws which we understand more and more as the years go by, and that there is no longer any need for God as part of our explanations. Soon, some say, science will be able to explain everything.

This chapter shows why such scientists' faith in the capacity of science to explain everything, is seriously misplaced, even for some very simple systems. This is the case, even in principle – in other words, there is no prospect of it ever becoming possible. This section sets out the basis of the belief in a purely mechanistic universe, but the next two sections will upset it.

My specific engineering background is relevant here. I have spent my working life in the analysis, design and control of dynamic systems, which are, put simply, any systems in which something moves, or changes, as time passes. That covers a great number of man-made electrical, mechanical, pneumatic, hydraulic and thermodynamic systems; but it also covers such things as the behavior of stock markets, and natural systems such as planetary motions, population changes, the blood flow around your body, a multitude of other systems within living things, and the behavior of the oceans, tectonic plates and weather systems – to name but a few.

Imagine that you have a dynamic system whose behavior you would like to predict. Let's say that it is a simple mechanical system, comprising a few interconnected masses, springs and dampers. To make this less abstract, it might, for example, be the suspension system of a road vehicle. In that case, the masses are those of the wheels and their mountings, and of the vehicle body and its load; the springs are the actual suspension springs, positioned between the wheel mountings and the vehicle body, and also the springiness of the tires between the road and the wheels; the dampers are the shock absorbers, which are mounted across the springs to control their oscillation and prevent the vehicle from bouncing wildly all over the place.

Let's say that you want to know how the vehicle will behave if it is subjected to a particular type of shock load, such as running over a brick in the road.

If you were to give me a specification of the system, in terms of the details of the various components and their positioning, I would then be able to do some mathematics, based on my knowledge of how such components behave. That would result in a set of equations describing how the system behaves. Such a set of equations is known as a *mathematical model* of the system.

It is also known as a *deterministic* model. If we know the present state of the system, which we call its 'initial conditions', a deterministic mathematical model allows us to predict the future behavior of the system, in response to any given disturbance, starting from those known initial conditions.

So, if you were also to tell me the 'initial conditions' of your system, in terms of such things as the positions and velocities of the various components just before the vehicle hits the brick in the road; and if you also told me the size and shape of the brick; then I could produce results, such as graphs, or animations, predicting the responses of every component in the system after the vehicle hits the brick.

If your initial information was correct, in terms of the components in the system and the initial conditions, then my results should be reasonably accurate because I have successfully done such things before, and I know the laws of nature that apply. For relatively simple systems, a deterministic model can work well, given sufficiently accurate information.

This is one way in which scientists investigate the behavior of real-world systems, and it is also how engineers evaluate the designs of new systems before they are even constructed. In such cases, the mathematical models of the systems are derived from the physics of the various elements to be used in building them. Note that we must have faith in the (un-provable) notion that the laws of physics are reliably constant, in order for this modeling technique to be reliable.

I can do exactly the same sort of exercise for any other type of engineering system. For example, for a simple electrical system comprising a few standard components, given the initial conditions in terms of the various voltages (potential differences, for technical readers) and currents in the system, their rates of change, and the details of a voltage or current signal which is going to disturb the system in some way, I could predict the resulting voltages and currents at any point in the system as time passes.

Even after working in such areas for many years, I still find the elegance of some of the mathematics a source of fascination. I referred to the beauty of mathematics earlier but, unfortunately, the beautiful mathematics generally crops up in situations that are too complicated for the non-expert to be able to appreciate it. The mathematicians and scientists are usually the only ones who are privileged to see it – it is one of the perks of the job! In this particular case though, it may be possible to give just an inkling of this type of elegance, the question being, where does it come from? Science doesn't know.

If we choose carefully the way in which we write the equations of such mathematical models, a perfectly consistent set of analogies can be established between the different types of physical system. For example, the simplest mathematical model describing the behavior of a rotating mechanical mass (a wheel, for example) can be absolutely identical, in form, to that describing an electrical capacitor (a component which stores electrical energy), even though they are completely different things. But it doesn't stop there. The model also looks identical in form to that of a sliding mass, that of a thermal system that stores heat energy, and that of the liquid level in a storage tank with varying flows in and out, for example.

The same applies to the other components in the different types of system. An electrical resistor's mathematical model (if you recall

Ohm's law from school – that's it) looks identical in form to a certain type of mechanical friction model, and to the model for the thermal resistance of a wall, and to that for the fluid resistance in a pipe. This means that, if one knows how to analyze one of these types of system, one effectively knows how to analyze them all, even though they are very different types of system.

The existence of elegance and beauty in the mathematics of the laws of nature is, to many people, yet another indication that those laws resulted from ideas in the Mind of God. There is no other known reason why there should be beauty in the mathematics. As usual, it could just be coincidence, but the number of those will be quite large by the end of this book.

Towards the end of the seventeenth century, Isaac Newton published his laws of motion, and his ideas that contributed to the mathematical field of calculus. These are the types of tool used in developing models such as the ones described above, and they work very well. It then seems that, since we can model simple systems, we can put those models together to model more complex ones, and so on, leading to the notion of the 'clockwork universe' mentioned at the start of this section. The universe is then sometimes said to be 'nothing but' a set of systems, simply following the laws of nature – if we understand the laws, we can ultimately understand the universe. We are back to the 'nothing buttery' of the previous chapter.

This is even taken, by some, to apply to our brains, and hence to our thoughts; then it really becomes the philosophy of determinism, rather than hard science. Philosophical determinism teaches that all states in the universe, including our brain states and the thoughts and actions arising from them, are completely determined by what has gone before – it describes an entirely clockwork universe. Donald MacKay called this philosophy 'machine-mindedness', since it reduces the universe, and you and me, to 'nothing but' machines.[12]

At its extreme, this philosophy can also lead to scientism, in which science is held to be the final arbiter of truth. This claims that the scientific method should be applied to everything, and that nothing is worth knowing if it can't be tested that way. There is certainly no need for God in such a world-view.

Setting aside these extra layers of supposition, there is nothing wrong with the word 'deterministic' when it is properly applied to mathematical models of dynamic systems. However, even then, there is sometimes a surprisingly large difference between the behavior of a deterministic model of a system, and the behavior of the real-world system that the model claims to represent. There are two nasty shocks lurking here for the supporters of the entirely clockwork universe.

## Uncertainty

The first nasty shock came from the development of quantum theory in the early twentieth century. Quantum theory generally applies in the sub-atomic world, where science investigates the fundamental particles that make up atoms and radiation. At this sub-atomic scale, it turns out that many of the laws of science that we apply to objects larger than atoms cease to apply, and quantum theory replaces them.

One of the discoveries of the quantum physicists was that there is a fundamental, unavoidable uncertainty about the precise state of matter. It turns out that some behavior of sub-atomic particles is not entirely predictable; not because we don't yet know how to do it, but because it is a fundamental aspect of nature. This behavior is described by laws of probability, rather than by absolute certainty.

For example, we can only know the probability that a sub-atomic particle is in a particular place, moving with a particular velocity. When we try actually to measure these things, the very act of trying to observe the system disturbs it and changes its behavior. It turns out that we can know the position of the particle, or its velocity, but not both at the same time. The more accurately we know one, the less accurately we can know the other (as formalized in Werner Heisenberg's Uncertainty Principle).

Usually, at the scale of everyday objects, these sub-atomic, probabilistic effects average out, to give the behavior described by the normal laws of nature. Nevertheless, because we can never hope accurately to know what is going on within atoms, there can be no complete mechanistic description of the universe. That means, in turn, that there is always the possibility of something surprising happening, however unlikely it might be.

As an example, radioactive uranium-235 is one of the 'clocks' used in radiometric dating. It has a half-life of 704 million years, meaning that half of the uranium-235 atoms in any given sample will have decayed (to thorium atoms) after 704 million years. After a further 704 million years, half of the remaining uranium-235 atoms will have decayed, and so on. However, it is impossible to predict when any particular atom will decay. It may be in the next second, or it may not be for billions of years. That is just one example of things about the universe that we can never know, however good our science becomes.

## Unpredictability

The second nasty shock was discovered, lurking in the background, in the last quarter of the nineteenth century. At that time some scientists began to suspect that unpredictability is built into some fundamental aspects of the way the universe operates, but the necessary techniques to follow up the ideas didn't become available until about a century later. This unpredictability operates at the scale of everyday systems that directly affect all our lives. As we shall see later, it may also be relevant to the question of how God might work in the world today.

The effects occur in a particular type of dynamic system, known as a 'chaotic system'; they are described by what has come to be known as chaos theory. Many chaotic systems have mathematical models that look entirely deterministic; there is nothing in those models to indicate that they will be anything other than well behaved. That's another reason why it was not until the middle of the twentieth century that scientists began to direct much attention towards them. Our more recent knowledge of chaotic systems has taught us that many real-world systems are inevitably going to be unpredictable in some aspects of their behavior.

One common reason for this is that the system may be incredibly sensitive, either to the slightest measurement error in its initial conditions, or to the slightest disturbance affecting it whilst it is in operation, or both. Even if the system itself is genuinely deterministic, and even if our mathematical model of it is perfectly accurate (which is, in itself, impossible), we still cannot know the initial conditions of the system, or the disturbances acting on it, with sufficient accuracy to be able to reliably predict its behavior over long periods of time. The actual behavior of the system will soon deviate, possibly in totally unexpected ways, from that which even a perfectly accurate model of the system predicts – there are examples shortly.

Together with the quantum uncertainty in sub-atomic systems, this inherently chaotic behavior of many large-scale systems has sounded the death knell for the dream of all-encompassing determinism; it is no longer allowable to automatically equate deterministic models with predictability of the future behavior of the real world.

The behavior of stock markets is a good everyday example of a chaotic system, but a classic example is that of long-term weather forecasting. As more and more weather data are gathered, the meteorologists and climatologists are continuously improving their mathematical models of how the atmosphere works, so that weather forecasting is getting better all the time. However, there is the fundamental problem that the atmosphere and its weather systems constitute a chaotic system. If our present understanding is correct, we shall never be able to produce an accurate long-range forecast of its behavior.

As an indication of the sensitivity of weather systems to tiny disturbances, one of the major contributors to our knowledge of chaotic systems, the meteorologist and mathematician Edward Lorenz, used the illustration that a flap of a butterfly's wings in Brazil could perhaps eventually result in a tornado in Texas. The general idea is that such a tiny effect as that due to a butterfly, in the wrong place at the wrong time, could lead to major effects later. This type of extreme sensitivity is now often called the 'Butterfly Effect'.

In my more advanced engineering lectures, I sometimes used a computer simulation of a fairly simple system, which clearly demonstrates such sensitivity to initial conditions. I have also used it successfully in talks to non-scientific audiences, so it's worth describing it here since understanding it will provide not only a numerical example of the sensitivity of a chaotic system, but also an illustration, later, of how God might be able to act in the world.

Imagine a triangle, drawn on a horizontal surface, and having equal sides each about half a meter long. Three identical, strong magnets are fixed to the surface, one at each point of the triangle. Suspended exactly over the center of the triangle of magnets is a two meter long pendulum, comprising a cord with an iron bob on the end.

The magnets attract the pendulum bob, but the length of the pendulum is such that it can swing over them without quite touching them. However, if the bob is pulled directly over one of the magnets and released, the magnet is sufficiently powerful to hold it there.

This pendulum therefore has four possible states in which it can come to rest. It can be 'captured' by any of the three magnets, or it can come to rest hanging vertically downwards over the center of the triangle – where the forces of attraction from the magnets are weak and, in any case, tend to cancel each other out.

Now imagine that you get hold of the pendulum bob and pull it sideways, away from the center of the triangle, say by approximately one meter, and then release it.

It will swing back over the triangle of magnets, past the center, and onwards, until it reverses and swings back towards you again, and so on, as a pendulum does. In doing so, it will pass nearer to some magnets than others, and the different forces of attraction from the magnets will have an effect on its trajectory. After a sequence of many oscillations around some, or all, of the three magnets, the pendulum will come to rest in one of the four possible positions – over one of the magnets, or in the center.

Now imagine that you again pull the pendulum sideways from the center of the triangle, until it is as near to the previous release point as you can possibly get it, and then release it again; what will happen?

The pendulum will initially follow a path almost identical to the previous one. That's what we would expect, because you were careful to try to release it from exactly the same position as before. However, you could never reposition it *exactly* where it had been in the first experiment, and the very slight difference in the second release position means that the effects from the magnets will be very slightly different this time.

As a result, after a few cycles of oscillation, the trajectory will gradually begin to diverge noticeably from that of the previous experiment. Eventually, it will become completely different, to the extent that the pendulum may well come to rest in a different one of its four possible rest states.

So, two different release positions, differing only by an amount so small that you couldn't avoid it, result in the pendulum coming to rest in two of its four possible rest states. It turns out that, for two other release positions, also differing by only a *very small* amount from the first two, the pendulum might come to rest in its other two possible rest states.

A surprise awaits us though, in the size of the "very small" differences in release position that are sufficient to cause the pendulum to come to rest in a completely different state. In the computer simulation, it is easy to find a release position that, together with three different small deviations from it, resulted in the pendulum bob coming to rest in each of the four possible positions. These four starting positions are all within *four millionths of a millimeter* of each other; that's four nanometers – approximately the distance your fingernails grow in four seconds.[18]

Even if you made some simple engineering effort to assist in re-positioning the pendulum really accurately, for example by setting up a jig against which you could push the bob each time, you would still not achieve that sort of accuracy in re-positioning it.

Intuitively, for a two meter pendulum pulled almost one meter sideways, differences of as little as that in the release position will be completely negligible. It is, after all, only about 0.000 000 4 of one percent of the sideways deflection; nevertheless it results in the most significant differences possible in the final state of this system.

In an even more impressive example of a chaotic system's sensitivity to initial conditions, the nuclear physicist and theologian John Polkinghorne calculates that, over the extremely short time interval of $10^{-10}$ seconds (one tenth of one billionth of a second – see this endnote for an explanation[19]), each molecule in the air around us will have about fifty collisions with its neighbors. He poses the question, "How accurately do we have to know things at the beginning in order to be able to predict how one of those molecules will be moving ... after its fifty collisions?"

He concludes that, in trying to predict the behavior of a molecule in the air after its fifty collisions, even after only a tenth of a billionth of a second, "We shall make a serious error in our calculation if we have failed to take into account the effect of an electron (the smallest particle of matter) on the other side of the observable universe (as far away as you can get) interacting with the air by means of gravitational attraction (the weakest of the forces of nature). In other words, even for a simple system like air, for a period which is a very tiny fraction of a second, its detailed behavior is absolutely unpredictable without literally universal knowledge."[20]

That last statement implies that we would need to know the position of every electron, in every atom in the universe, in order to stand any chance of successfully making the calculation.

A different aspect of chaotic systems is illustrated by a very simple equation that is used as the basis of some mathematical models of animal population dynamics (the way in which populations change year by year). The model used here contains only two parameters – the present population, and a number, $F$, which defines how the population will have changed at the next time point of interest (for example, after one year).[21]

For some chosen population 'now', if $F$ is given a small value, and the equation is applied repeatedly many times, so as to simulate the passing of many years, then the population eventually decays to zero (simulating the running out of food, for example).

If the value of $F$ is *very gradually* increased and, for each new value of $F$, the above procedure is repeated, a particular value of $F$ will eventually be found at which the population settles to a constant, non-zero number of animals, rather than decaying to zero. This value of $F$ is very sensitive – the value which results in the non-zero steady state, will require an increase of only a tiny fraction of one percent from the previous value, which caused the population to decay to zero.

If the value of $F$ is further gradually increased, and the above procedure is repeated, the real surprises begin. At some very specific value of $F$, the population will settle into an oscillation between two alternate values. After one year there will be a certain population, after the next year, a different population, and these two values will then keep appearing, alternately, as the years pass.

If the value of $F$ is further gradually increased, a specific value of $F$ will then be found at which the population will settle into an oscillation between four alternate values, repeating every four years.

As $F$ is further increased, this doubling of the oscillation period keeps happening at very precise values of $F$. The increase in $F$ between successive doublings gets shorter each time, until a precise value of $F$ is found at which a non-repeating, apparently random, oscillation sets in, and the population never settles into a pattern. This is 'chaotic' behavior.

For higher values of $F$, various other behaviors then exhibit themselves, in which repeating patterns re-emerge every so often, only to be followed by more chaotic oscillations as $F$ is then even further increased.[22]

Enough has probably been said to indicate why scientists initially found it hard to accept that a system represented by a very simple equation could produce such complex and unpredictable behavior. Nevertheless, investigations showed that, in addition to animal populations, many other real-world systems do exhibit this type of behavior, including stock market behavior and weather systems. For a readable description of this area, see James Gleick's book, "*Chaos*".[23]

Nobody expected this kind of behavior from a simple deterministic model, and the consequence is that any model that looks deterministic, if it has certain particular characteristics,[24] may start to exhibit unexpected behavior. I used to teach a course in which I told my students at least a little about the types of system potentially capable of this sort of behavior. Unfortunately, such courses are now a rarity at undergraduate level, due to the combination of the reduction of class-contact time for students, and the pressure on the curriculum due to inclusion of other topics.

## Why does this matter?

Although some inconvenient real-world aspects of dynamic systems, as exemplified above, are still at least mentioned in some courses, many graduates from science and engineering courses will never come across them. They will leave university believing that the systems of the universe can be modeled entirely deterministically, and that if we could know the conditions of all those systems now, then we could predict all the universe's future states.

Unfortunately, it's just not true; the uncertainty of quantum physics and the unpredictable behavior of chaotic systems have seen to that. Reductionism and scientism, in these senses, are dead. Later we shall consider what all this might have to do with religion.

## Chapter 4  Creation

In Chapter One, in the section headed, "Different types of explanation", there was a brief description of the current scientific view of creation, and a very brief comparison with the version at the beginning of the Christian Bible (the book of Genesis). This chapter looks in more detail at the very early moments of the universe, whilst the following two chapters look at the subsequent evolution of stars and galaxies, and the evolution of life on Earth. After all that, we shall briefly look at the biblical version again.

### How did we arrive at twenty-first century science?

Modern science is based on observation of the world around us, and the sustained effort to analyze and explain what we observe by using the scientific method described in Chapter One. It dates from the sixteenth and seventeenth centuries – though other interpretations are available.

Aristotle (384-322 BC), taught that Earth was at the center of the universe, and everything revolved around it in circular orbits arranged in concentric spheres. This idea held sway for some 1,900 years, but then ideas began to change rapidly.

Firstly, based on careful observations of the motions of the planets, Nicolaus Copernicus (1473-1543) put forward a coherent theory that The Sun must be at the center of our solar system, rather than Earth. He also explained that Earth must rotate on its own axis once a day, and he explained other observations in terms of the tilt of Earth's axis. Some of these ideas had been suggested in earlier times, but Copernicus put them on a 'modern' footing.

Galileo Galilei (1564-1642) built himself a version of the newly invented telescope. With it, he observed four of the moons orbiting

Jupiter (now called the Galilean Moons in his honor), and also the phases of Venus.[25] This convinced him, and anyone else prepared to take a look, that Copernicus had to be correct. Since Jupiter had its own moons, for example, it obviously could not be the case that everything revolved around Earth.

Johannes Kepler (1571-1630) realized that the orbits of the planets around The Sun must be elliptical, rather than circular, in order to make sense of some of the details of their relative motions. Based purely upon careful observations of the planets, he formulated three mathematical laws, describing various aspects of planetary motion.

When Isaac Newton (1643-1727) developed his gravitational theory, he used it to analytically derive the orbits of the planets, and he discovered that two of Kepler's laws were spot-on, whilst the third needed only a slight modification. This is the sort of science that gives confidence in the resulting theories. Here were two fundamentally different approaches to a problem, which gave the same results. One approach fitted a mathematical description to match a set of observations, the other analytically derived the results expected from the physics, based on theory, and confirmed that the observations agreed.

In fact, although Newton's theory was by far the best that existed at that time, he was aware of some remaining small discrepancies between the predictions of his theory, and actual observations of the planets. He suggested that the "finger of God" must adjust the orbits from time to time, to keep things running correctly. About 230 years later, Einstein's general theory of relativity removed these discrepancies; Newton had fallen into what we would now call the 'god of the gaps' trap, described earlier.

The French mathematician, Pierre-Simon Laplace was born about twenty years after Newton's death and, amongst many other things, developed a famous mathematical transform theorem, widely-used in my own line of work. He also developed his own theory of the motion of the planets.

On one occasion, Laplace was presented to the emperor Napoleon. Napoleon apparently knew that Newton had invoked the "finger of God" to correct small deviations of the planets in order to keep their orbits stable, so he asked Laplace why his theory of the universe made no mention of the Creator of the universe. Laplace is famously said to have replied, "Sir, I had no need of that hypothesis." So, in Laplace's mind, God had apparently been ousted from the gap corresponding to knowledge of why dynamic systems behave as they do – but then,

Laplace didn't know about chaotic systems (as introduced in the previous chapter)!

Newton's most important work, in terms of developing the modern scientific approach, was probably his work in optics. He refined optical experiments to very high levels of accuracy over many years and, when that work was published in 1704, it finally established the power of relating theory to observation and vice versa.

## In the beginning – why the 'big bang' idea?

In the field of astronomy, as the years passed, scientists realized that most of the objects that they observed in the night sky were stars, similar to our Sun. However, as telescopes improved, they also observed other objects, which originally just looked like smears of light rather than points.

By the beginning of the twentieth century, the best telescopes had revealed that some of these strange objects had identifiable shapes, such as spirals. They were called nebulae, and were generally thought to be areas, fairly nearby in astronomical terms, in which new stars were being formed. We now know that these are galaxies other than our own but, at the beginning of the twentieth century, it was still generally thought that the Milky Way (our own galaxy) was actually the entire universe, containing everything visible in the night sky.

In 1912, an astronomer, Vesto Slipher, was investigating the characteristics of light coming from stars. He discovered that the light coming from the nebulae had similar characteristics to starlight, so he confirmed that the nebulae must, indeed, contain stars; but he went further.

When starlight is split into a spectrum (as when shining sunlight through a prism) and examined carefully, it is found to contain characteristic patterns of dark lines. Slipher noticed that, in the spectra of light coming from most of the nebulae, these patterns of lines were shifted towards the red end of the spectrum, when compared with the same patterns of lines in the spectra of 'normal' stars. He recorded the amounts of red shift for many of the nebulae known at the time, and scientists began to think about what this might imply.

You will probably have noticed the way in which an emergency vehicle siren, or the engine note of a fast car or motorcycle, falls in pitch (frequency) as it passes you. That is because the sound waves from the vehicle are compressed in front of it as it comes towards you, raising their frequency, but they become stretched out behind it as it moves away from you, so the frequency then drops; this is called Doppler shift.

The frequency of light waves coming from a moving object behaves in a similar way. If an object is coming towards you its light is shifted towards the higher-frequency (blue) end of the spectrum, if it is moving away, its light is shifted towards the lower-frequency (red) end of the spectrum. The greater the speed, the greater the frequency shift. At everyday speeds, the shifts in light color are so small that we don't notice them.

The red shifts, measured in the light from the nebulae, therefore indicated that the nebulae were moving away from us.[26] Some of them seemed to be moving away at enormously high velocities – large red shifts, representing thousands of kilometers per second, which was something of a puzzle at the time.

In the early 1920s, another astronomer, Edwin Hubble, using the best telescope in the world, was studying the Andromeda spiral nebula, which we now call the Andromeda galaxy. An expert observer, Milton Humason, assisted Hubble in making the required observations.

Hubble was interested in measuring the distances to stars known as Cepheid variables, which oscillate very regularly in size,[27] and are extremely useful to astronomers. Their periods of oscillation can be measured by observing them through a telescope and timing them, and those periods are related to how bright the stars actually are – not how bright they appear from Earth, having been dimmed by the distance in between.

By discovering the actual brightness of a Cepheid variable star in that way, and then measuring how bright it appears to be from Earth, it is possible to calculate how far away it is.[28] If the variable star is in another galaxy, then the calculated distance to the variable star also gives us the distance to the galaxy containing it.

As a result of Hubble's analysis, he discovered that the Andromeda spiral nebula was, literally, an astronomical distance away from us; much farther away than the entire size of the universe was thought to be at that time. He also discovered that the Andromeda nebula contained an astronomical number of stars. He had identified the first galaxy other than our own. He called it, and other nebulae that were similarly discovered to be separate galaxies, "island universes".

If you are fortunate enough to have been in an area well away from light pollution, you may have seen a diffuse milky band running across the night sky. It is actually a swathe of a huge number of stars, and is very impressive even when viewed through everyday binoculars. It has been observed since ancient times, and is known as the Milky Way. Hubble realized that the Milky Way is also a galaxy, and that our solar system is actually a part of it. When we look at the Milky Way in the night sky, we are actually looking towards the center of our own galaxy, where the density of stars is the greatest.

Hubble and Humason made measurements of the distances to about a hundred galaxies, and then Hubble decided to compare those measurements to Slipher's data of the redshifts associated with them. He realized two things. Firstly, the fact that the light from almost all of the galaxies was red-shifted meant that all those galaxies are moving away from us. Secondly, the red shift became greater, the farther away a galaxy was from us, which, as we shall see, was an extremely significant observation.

He also discovered that the same was true of movements between other pairs of galaxies – almost every galaxy was moving away from every other galaxy, at speeds proportional to the distances between each pair. This relationship was published in 1929, and became known as Hubble's law even though, as we shall see shortly, it had been predicted earlier. It led Hubble to wonder whether the universe might have started in a 'big bang' – though that name wasn't to be introduced for another twenty years. The reasoning goes as follows.

Imagine, for a moment, that all the galaxies were formed in an instant, exploding outwards from a single point. Let's think about the motion of two of those galaxies, A and B.

If Galaxy A is moving twice as fast as Galaxy B, then Galaxy A travels twice as far as Galaxy B in any given amount of time. Given that they started from the same point, at any time Galaxy A will therefore be twice as far from the starting point as Galaxy B.

As time passes, both galaxies continue to move away from the starting point, and Galaxy A will always be twice as far from the starting point as Galaxy B, so the distance between the two galaxies also increases as time passes.

When Hubble discovered that the galaxies that were travelling faster were a long way away from us, whilst the galaxies that were travelling slower were nearer to us, the scenario of the previous three paragraphs suggested itself to him. He realized that if he effectively reversed the 'movie' of the outward expansion of the galaxies, by running it backwards in time, all the galaxies would then move closer together.

He found that, if time could be run in reverse, all the galaxies would, indeed, converge onto one location, several billion years ago. Over the years since his discovery, successive refinements of that time have been made and we now believe that the universe exploded into being, from a single point, a little over 13.7 billion years ago, and has been expanding ever since.

Since almost all the galaxies seem to be receding from us, that description might seem to suggest that our galaxy must be at the center of the universe, but that isn't the case. Imagine travelling in a train, and overtaking another train. If you watch the other train, and imagine yourself to be stationary, you effectively see the other train moving away from you. A person sitting on the other train sees you moving away from them at exactly the same speed.

The same is true of the galaxies. Wherever we look in the universe, we see other galaxies receding from us, but so would observers in any other galaxy – we are not in any privileged location. A common analogy in thinking about this is to imagine a ball of currant-bun mixture, expanding as it cooks. As the mixture expands, it carries the currants with it, and they all move apart from each other. If you could stand on any one of the currants in the mixture, you would see all the others moving away from you.

The big drawback of the currant-bun analogy is that the bun is obviously expanding into the space inside the oven. The expansion of the universe is not like that, because space itself was also compressed into the single point at the big bang. Space has been expanding ever since, but it is not expanding into anything, as there is nothing for it to expand into. It is space itself that is expanding, and carrying the galaxies with it.

We must think of the currant bun mixture as space itself, and the currants as the galaxies, and forget about anything outside the ball of bun mixture. Then, as the currant bun expands, the currants move *with* the mixture, not through it. In exactly the same way, as the universe expands, the galaxies generally move *with* space, not through it. The analogy of sitting on one of the currants, and seeing all the others moving away from you, then illustrates that the large-scale behavior of the universe looks the same, no matter from where you choose to view it.

Perhaps the hardest thing to grasp is that, according to the big bang theory, *everything* began in that instant. All the matter of the universe came into existence in an instant, at that single, incredibly dense point, mathematically known as a 'singularity'. Space itself also came into existence in that point. If you can cope with that, even more confusingly, time began at that instant too; the endnote briefly explains why we believe that to be the case.[29]

There are 'local' exceptions to Hubble's law. In some relatively closely bound groups of galaxies, local gravitational effects of attraction between the galaxies overcome the normal tendency of galaxies to be moving apart. For example, the Milky Way and the Andromeda galaxy are quite close in astronomical terms, and both contain a lot of mass – both are larger than the average galaxy, with Andromeda being larger than the Milky Way.

According to the physicist and cosmologist Paul Davies, as a result of gravitational attraction the Milky Way and Andromeda are moving towards each other at about 130 kilometers (81 miles) every second.[30] We are heading for a collision, but it won't happen for a few billion years yet.

Even including such local anomalies, observations are in very good agreement with the theory of an expanding universe, wherever we look. There are also other, independent, indications that the big bang theory is correct.

## What other evidence is there for the big bang?

Apart from Hubble's law, and its implications, there is plenty of other evidence that supports the big bang theory of creation. Three pieces of extra evidence are introduced in this section and the next. One is based on theoretical mathematical analysis, one on nuclear physics, and one on a completely different type of observation of the visible universe. That gives us four pieces of reliable evidence, from different parts of science, using different types of analysis, all of which are in agreement. The evidence in favor of the big bang theory is very strong.

The first person to demonstrate that the big bang theory was supported by independent mathematical analysis was the Belgian physics professor and priest, Georges Lamaître. This was in 1927, so Lamaître actually envisaged something like Hubble's law and the expanding universe, before Hubble's work was published. At that time, most of Lamaître's fellow scientists instinctively disliked the idea of a moment of creation, rather than a universe that had always existed. In some ways, of course, it does point to a Creator, and moves the debate towards the religious camp. It is interesting that the first theoretical proponent of the big bang theory of creation was religious; he certainly felt no need to steer clear of it on the grounds of his religion, as some do today.

Since Einstein's general theory of relativity is our best gravitational theory, it is the theory used to investigate the evolution of the structure of the universe. Lamaître found a solution to Einstein's equations, which described the big bang universe very well; so did others, including Einstein himself, but Lamaître was the first to suggest that it corresponded with the reality of the evolution of the universe. Since general relativity is so well-tested, and very appropriate to this task, the agreement between observation and relativity theory, as to the timing and existence of a big bang moment of creation, is strong evidence that it actually happened.

Despite the type of evidence described above, some scientists still disliked the big bang theory of creation on philosophical grounds – they simply disliked the idea that everything had a definite beginning, including time. Some scientists still dislike it today, though most do agree that the theory gives the best fit between the observed facts and the analysis.

Perhaps the best-known opponent of the big bang theory was Fred Hoyle, who championed a theory of steady-state creation. That theory suggested that the universe had been expanding forever, and that matter was continuously being created to populate the new space made available by the expansion. In fact, it was Hoyle who coined the term "big bang", during a BBC radio broadcast in which he was arguing against the big bang theory.

Until a few years ago, there was a popular theory amongst scientists that the expansion of the universe might slow down, and then reverse, so that all the matter in the universe would be attracted together by gravity and would eventually end up at a single point again, in a 'big crunch'. That might then 'bounce' into another big bang, and so the cycle might continue.

If that were true, perhaps it could have been going on forever, and our big bang was just the start of a new cycle. However, in the 1990s it was discovered that the rate of expansion of the universe is actually increasing, and the idea of 'dark energy' was introduced to explain this. We don't yet understand what this dark energy is, but it is thought to exist everywhere in space, and to contribute a large proportion of all the mass-energy in the universe.

If that is true, then the universe may well expand for ever, making a series of previous big bangs look rather unlikely, and increasing the probability that *the* big bang was, indeed, the beginning of time and space.

When speaking on this topic, I am sometimes asked, "What happened before the big bang?" Unfortunately, either the question is meaningless, or we just can't know for sure.[31]

The evidence suggests that time began at the moment of the big bang. In that case, "before the big bang" simply didn't exist. The question then contains a category mistake, similar to asking, "What lies to the North of the North Pole?" If you reach the North Pole, then taking a step in any direction takes you South; the direction "North" simply has no meaning. Similarly, from the big bang, the only direction time goes is forwards; there is no "before".

On the other hand, if our present thinking is wrong, in the sense that there was something before the big bang, the fact that the big bang still happened means that we can never see back beyond it. Our mathematics and physics run into trouble once we have worked our way backwards to the moment of the big bang and, as we shall see in the next section, we cannot even make any physical observations of anything that happened in the first 380,000 years of the universe's existence.

Before ending this chapter, we shall look at two more pieces of evidence that support the validity of the big bang theory, one of which finally persuaded Fred Hoyle that it was correct. These require a little more background, but they are worth mentioning because they demonstrate that anyone who wants to deny this theory has really got his work cut out.

## What happened in the very early universe?

One aspect of a good scientific theory is that it might make predictions about as-yet-unobserved phenomena, which can then be investigated. If they are then duly discovered, as predicted, that tends to be very strong evidence that the theory is on the right track. This happened more than once in the further development of the big bang theory of creation.

Once the big bang theory had been accepted by an appropriate number of respectable scientists, people began to think about how the universe, as we now observe it, might have developed from that initial beginning.

Because the very early universe contained all the energy necessary for the universe to develop over billions of years, compressed into almost zero space, it was unbelievably hot. In fact, according to John Barrow,[32] scientists have calculated that the initial temperature may have been as much as $10^{32}$K. (If you would like a brief explanation of the notation for large numbers, such as the "$10^{32}$", which means 1 followed by 32 zeros, see this endnote.[33] For the Kelvin temperature scale, represented by the "K", take a look at this endnote.[34])

When the big bang occurred, the very early universe was so hot that matter as we know it simply couldn't exist – everything is 'vaporized' at that kind of temperature. In fact, it was too hot even for atoms to be able to hold together, so it will have been a seething mass of fundamental sub-atomic particles.

On Earth, the highest temperatures we can generate are in particle accelerators, the most powerful being the Large Hadron Collider (LHC), at CERN, near Geneva,[35] in which particles can be accelerated to within a tiny fraction of one percent of the speed of light. At those speeds, two beams of particles are made to collide, which disintegrates the particles, and results in a shower of more-fundamental particles that can be studied using several sophisticated detectors. This is how scientists investigate the fundamental structure of matter, and these are the kinds of particles that would have constituted the matter existing in the universe very shortly after the big bang.[36]

Physicists believe that, the tiniest fraction of a second after the big bang, the rate of expansion of the universe was colossally high. For a very short time it was faster than the speed of light.[37] That brief period, of faster-than-light expansion of space, is the reason why we now cannot observe some parts of the universe; they are now so far away from us, and receding so quickly, that light from them has not been able reach us.

## The proportion of helium in the universe

You might have noticed that, if you spray an aerosol can for a long time, it gets cold. Similarly, you might have noticed a thick layer of ice crystals on the valves and pipes around gas cylinders outside industrial premises or hospitals. The reason for this is that, as gases expand, they cool down. As the universe has expanded, it has cooled in the same sort of way.

At first, since the rate of expansion was extremely high, so was the rate of cooling. By the time the universe was only about one microsecond (one millionth of a second) old, the temperature had fallen to about 10 trillion degrees.

The fundamental component of each chemical element is the atom. Atoms are made up of a very dense nucleus, containing particles known as protons and neutrons, surrounded by a number of orbiting electrons. The number of protons in an atom's nucleus determines which chemical element it is.[38] Because the nucleus is so dense, it contains almost all of the atom's mass. Most of an atom, where the extremely tiny electrons are orbiting, is empty space.

Once the temperature of the very early universe had fallen to 10 trillion degrees, nuclei of the lightest element, hydrogen, whose nucleus is just a single proton, could form because the appropriate fundamental particles could be bound into a stable proton at that temperature.

By the time the universe was about three minutes old, the temperature had fallen to 'only' about 750 million degrees, when the nuclei of the next two elements in the series, helium and lithium, could form by various collisions and nuclear reactions between hydrogen nuclei. These are called nucleosynthesis reactions, as nuclei of heavier elements are built up (synthesized) by reacting those of lighter elements.

The nuclear physics of such reactions predicts that the proportions of helium and hydrogen formed in these reactions should be about 23 percent helium, with most of the remainder being hydrogen – only small quantities of lithium would form because the lithium nucleus is not very stable.

It turns out that the oldest things we can observe in the universe do, indeed, contain the predicted proportion of helium. Martin Rees[39] points out that, "No star, galaxy or nebula has been found where helium is less abundant than [23 – 24 percent]". From Chapter One, we know that second-generation stars were formed from the remains of exploded first-generation stars. Those first-generation stars would have manufactured some extra helium internally during their lives, so the more recent second-generation stars would be expected to contain a little more than 23 percent helium.

Rees also points out that The Sun contains about 27 percent helium in its outer layers, the extra three or four percent being, "just about what would have been made" by the previous generation of stars, from whose remains our Sun formed.

These are further extremely good pointers to the fact that the big bang theory is correct. No other theory has been discovered which would result in sufficient helium in the universe to match the observations.

## The cosmic microwave background radiation

Only a few minutes after the big bang, the temperature became too low for nucleosynthesis reactions to continue, resulting in the hydrogen, helium, and just a little lithium described in the previous section. However, the temperature was still extremely high in everyday terms, to the extent that electrons were still moving too energetically to be captured by the nuclei of hydrogen, helium and lithium to form proper atoms – they remained bare nuclei at this stage.

The clouds of energetic particles flying around the early universe meant that any photons of energy (such as light) emitted in the universe would very soon collide with other particles and be scattered. Therefore no visible image of anything could form, and the early universe was effectively opaque. This situation persisted for about the first 380,000 years, as the universe continued to expand and cool.

After about 380,000 years, the temperature had fallen to 3,000K. That is a significant temperature, because electrons then had energies sufficiently low to allow them to be captured by the nuclei of hydrogen, helium and lithium to form conventional atoms. The mopping up of electrons into atoms allowed space to become transparent. Therefore radiation commensurate with a temperature of 3,000K could now exist throughout the entire universe.

As the universe has continued to expand since then, the temperature has continued to fall. In 1948, Ralph Alpher and Robert Herman estimated that the further expansion of the universe, in the billions of years since the big bang, would mean that we should now be able to observe this radiation, as a kind of signature of the big bang, at a temperature of about 5K, wherever we look in the sky. Later refinements amended that figure to just below 3K. These temperatures are characteristic of microwaves, so this was a prediction that there should be low-temperature microwave radiation visible in all directions.

In 1965, Arno Penzias and Robert Wilson were working with a large antenna for receiving microwaves. The experiment they were performing required the detection of very weak signals, and therefore it was necessary to eliminate all interference from their receiving equipment. They took great pains to achieve this but, even so, a background 'hiss' troubled them 24 hours per day, and did not vary as they pointed their antenna at different parts of the sky. They had discovered the cosmic microwave background radiation.[40]

I recall, in the 1970s, being fascinated by the 'snow' on the old analogue television screens after transmission of programs had ended late in the evening. That fascination arose from the fact that a small part of the electrical 'noise' was due to the microwave background – I was watching the echo of the big bang!

Since then, satellites (such as COBE launched in 1989, WMAP launched in 2001, and the Planck Surveyor launched in 2009) have mapped the background radiation ever more accurately in all parts of the sky. There are only extremely small variations between different areas of the sky, but those are necessary, as we shall see in the next chapter, if galaxies were to be able to form. The distribution is exactly as expected, and this background radiation is perhaps the best independent piece of evidence for the correctness of the big bang theory.

The cumulative evidence for the big bang theory, coming from diverse areas such as those described in this chapter, is extremely strong, and has not been matched by any other theory of creation. As a result, most scientists now believe that the big bang theory is correct. In the next chapter, we'll briefly describe the evolution of the universe following the big bang.

## Religious aspects of the big bang

This chapter has presented some of the ideas that constitute convincing evidence for the big bang theory of creation, accepted by the majority of scientists. If religious creation beliefs seem to suggest otherwise, some work is necessary to square up the differences between the two. Unfortunately, I am only qualified to comment on the Judeo-Christian version.

I find the big bang theory very helpful, in that it does point to a moment of creation – the precise reason why some scientists initially opposed it, until the evidence became too strong. The difficulties for some religious people might then lie in the fact that the big bang happened so long ago.

Paul Davies[30] points out that the idea of time beginning in the big bang would not have been surprising to some of the ancient thinkers we have already mentioned. For example, he quotes Augustine as having written, "The world was made with time, not in time", and points out that, "Augustine's God is a being who transcends time, a being located outside time altogether, and responsible for creating time as well as space and matter. Thus Augustine skillfully avoided the problem of why the creation happened at that moment rather than some other, earlier moment. *There were no earlier moments* [Davies' italics]." He also reminds us that Augustine wrote his comment in the fifth century. My understanding is that, when Augustine wrote "the world", he would have meant the known universe.

If you are religious, and feel inclined to deny the big bang theory on religious grounds, I understand. However, my own view was that it made more sense to re-evaluate the interpretation of that part of my religion that made me inclined to do that. In the case of Christianity, accepting that Genesis is not a science text is the key to that, as discussed at the end of Chapter One.

Also, the view that the big bang, followed by the events described in the next chapter, was God's chosen way of allowing the universe to make itself, seems to be entirely consistent with mainstream Christianity. We shall be returning to that idea later.

There is one more general point worth making here; this version of it comes from John Barrow.[32] He asks, "If the universe did begin at a singularity ... [and] if space and time did not exist before that singular beginning, how do we account for the laws of gravitation, or of logic, or mathematics? Did they exist 'before' the singularity? If so – and we seem to grant as much when we apply mathematics and logic to the singularity itself – then we must admit to a rationality larger than the material universe."

The implication that the laws of nature were 'already there' when the big bang occurred seems sound, and it also seems sensible to suggest that it is God, who is not constrained by our notions of time and space, who was responsible for those laws, and who is Barrow's "rationality larger than the material universe".

## Chapter 5   The Structure of the Universe

This chapter is included partly because the sheer number of galaxies, their scale, and some of the amazing things that occur inside them, contribute to our sense of awe and wonder at creation. But there is a more serious purpose – it also prepares the ground for some later discussions about the 'fine-tuning' of the universe.

There are very many things that had to happen in order for the universe to evolve the way it has, and for us to be here to investigate it. Science has discovered that several of those things were extremely improbable, and depended on some very finely tuned 'coincidences' occurring, sometimes one after another. Had some of those situations been ever so slightly different from the way they were, then we would not be here to think about it.

For me, and many other religious scientists, such discoveries act as further pointers towards the Mind of God behind the universe but, before we can enter into a discussion about that, we need to understand some of this fine-tuning.

Before that, as a temporary diversion from the science, and without any further comment, here are a couple of the astronomical wonders to which the evolution of the universe has led. These represent the kinds of thing that can continue to take our breath away when we think about them, even though we have known about them for many years.

The Hubble Space Telescope (named in honor of Edwin Hubble, whose work we mentioned earlier) has given us some mind-blowing pictures. As one example, a well-publicized image known as "The Pillars of Creation", captured as long ago as 1995, remains one of my favorites.[41] We still use the word 'nebulae' for large accumulations of gas, dust and stars that are within our own galaxy, and this image shows three dense pillars of dust and gas in the Eagle Nebula, in the constellation Serpens.

At the ends of the pillars can be seen the light from new stars, born from the accumulation of some of the dust and gas under the influence of gravity. Other bright, new stars are visible in the image. The Eagle Nebula is about 6,500 light years from Earth,[42] so the star-formation in the image was actually taking place about 6,500 years ago, though its light is only just reaching us.

To me, the most awe-inspiring thing about this image is the sheer scale of the gas clouds; the length of the largest pillar in the photograph is about four light years. Just think about that for a moment. During each second ticked off by your watch, light travels 300,000 km (186,000 miles). That's about 7.5 times around Earth's equator – every second. In one minute, light would travel around Earth's equator about 450 times, but it still takes light about four *years* to travel along that pillar of gas and dust.

The distance between The Sun and Earth would fit over a quarter of a million times into the length of that pillar. Alternatively, our entire solar system, represented by the average 'diameter' of the orbit of Neptune, would fit along the pillar over four thousand times.

Given the vast scale of the Eagle Nebula, it is perhaps hard to realize that, actually, this is just one unimaginably small part of the whole of creation. Even in terms of our galaxy, the Eagle Nebula is tiny, and this four-light-year-long pillar pales into insignificance compared with the 100,000 light year diameter of the Milky Way itself.

Then, it turns out that the Milky Way is just one of perhaps 100 billion galaxies, separated by unimaginable distances in space – and that is just in the part of the universe visible to us.

Another amazing astronomical wonder is the pulsar. These are some of the most impressive stellar objects in the known universe. We begin with a neutron star, which is the core of an old star, several times more massive than The Sun. It has consumed all its fuel and lost its outer layers in a supernova explosion, as described later in this chapter. The star's collapsed core is amongst the densest forms of matter known. It comprises almost entirely neutrons – so this is basically matter with all the empty space squeezed out. On earth, one teaspoonful of neutron star material would weigh over one billion tons. A commonly quoted analogy is that this kind of density is roughly equivalent to compressing Earth's seven billion people into the volume of a sugar cube.

Neutron stars can spin remarkably rapidly. As a post-supernova star collapses to form the neutron star, its diameter decreases. Just as the rotational speed of a skater's spin increases as she draws in her arms, so the rotational speed of a collapsing star increases as its diameter reduces.

Some neutron stars also have very strong magnetic fields that, in ways still not properly understood, have the effect of focusing radiation from the spinning star into a narrow beam. These beams, due to the star's rotation, may sweep across Earth like the beam from an old rotating lighthouse lens, or the spinning light reflector on the roof of an emergency vehicle. We therefore observe such beams as regular pulses of radiation, each time the rotation of the star sweeps the beam past us.

Such rotating neutron stars, emitting what we observe as pulses of radiation, are called pulsars. The huge mass of the pulsar means that the period of rotation is extremely regular (think of it as a flywheel), and some pulsars keep time almost as well as our best atomic clocks, over the time periods for which we are able to observe them.

In their book *Why Does E=mc²*, Brian Cox and Jeff Forshaw[43] tell us that, "Some known pulsars are approaching twice the mass of our Sun, measure only 20 kilometers in diameter, and spin more than five hundred times every second." Thinking about that for a while may make your head spin at the same kind of rate.

Several books have been filled with descriptions of the wonders of the universe, but we must return to our story. As we look around the universe with our best telescopes and other instruments, the overall structure that we now see, is of matter gathered together into clusters, and even super-clusters, of galaxies. On the largest scale, the clusters are fairly evenly distributed throughout space, with enormous dark voids between them. Each cluster is made up of individual galaxies, such as our Milky Way. Those galaxies, in turn, contain billions upon billions of stars, and other matter that we cannot see because it emits no light, but it is believed to contribute a very much greater proportion of the mass of the universe than all the visible stars.

The galaxies within the clusters are not so evenly distributed though. Some of them tend to group together under gravitational attraction. For example, our Milky Way belongs to such a group of galaxies. It is not strictly-defined, but this 'Local Group', as it is called, is generally taken to include anything within a distance of about four million light years from us – that's about 40 times the diameter of the Milky Way – in all directions. It comprises some 30 or 40 galaxies, including the Andromeda galaxy (larger than the Milky Way) and the Triangulum galaxy (about half the size of the Milky Way – a fairly average size for galaxies). All the other galaxies in the Local Group are relatively small, including the Large and Small Magellanic Clouds, both of which are visible to the naked eye only because they are relatively near to us.

In fact, the two Magellanic Clouds, together with Andromeda and, some say, Triangulum, are the only four celestial bodies visible to the naked eye in the night sky, other than The Moon, the planets in our own solar system, and stars in our own galaxy. Even then, you need to be far away from light pollution to have any chance of seeing those galaxies without binoculars or, preferably, a telescope.

It is interesting to consider how the galaxies came to be arranged as we see them now. In the previous chapter, we came across the cosmic microwave background radiation, and saw that it is very evenly spread across the sky. However, in the early universe, if all the matter had been perfectly evenly spread out, then there would have been no tendency for matter to clump together, under the influence of gravity, into the stars, galaxies and clusters of galaxies which we now see. Instead, each particle would have experienced the same gravitational attraction from its neighbors, as each other particle, and would therefore have stayed where it was relative to its neighbors.

In order to result in the distribution of matter we see in the universe today, there must have been some slight variations in density of the early universe from place to place. Those would have resulted in slightly uneven patterns of gravitational attraction, pulling particles in one direction or another relative to their neighbors, and thus pulling groups of particles together. Once a group of particles began to accumulate, the concentration of mass in that location would clearly increase, so it would then be able to exert a greater gravitational attraction on remaining nearby particles, to draw them in too.

Perhaps you can imagine that, if this effect was too small, the universe would have remained 'flat', whilst, if it was too great, matter might have aggregated too quickly, into very large accretions, compared with what we actually see. In either case, we would not now be here; this is the kind of 'fine-tuning' phenomenon about which we shall be thinking later.

In spite of this, the microwave background really is extremely smooth. Paul Davies says that, once the effect of Earth's motion through the background radiation (at about 600 kilometers per second) is accounted for, "To roughly one part in 100,000 there is no variation across the sky."[30]

To give you an idea of how smooth that is, if Earth only had surface variations of about one part in 100,000, the highest 'mountain' would only be 64 meters high; less than the wingspan of a Jumbo Jet, and this includes any of the height variation that might be under a (very shallow) sea.

These tiny variations in the background radiation represent tiny variations in density in the early universe.[44] As described above, there would therefore have been a tendency for places that were marginally denser to become even denser, by gravitationally attracting matter from the less dense areas nearby. The less dense areas would therefore, in turn, become even less dense.

As the universe expanded, these initial areas of slightly higher density evolved into the clusters of galaxies that we now observe to be evenly distributed throughout the universe. Were it not for those tiny initial fluctuations in density, represented by variations of only one part in 100,000 in the background radiation, there would now be no structure to the universe: no galaxies, no stars, no planets, no life, and no humans. Later, we consider whether God might have a role in all of this.

As each cluster of galaxies became a separate region of matter, gravity continued to act on marginally more dense regions within each cluster, with the result that they condensed into the individual galaxies that now form the cluster. Locally, the effects of gravitational attraction were sometimes sufficiently strong to overcome the general expansion of space, which resulted in nearby galaxies moving towards each other, as in the case of Andromeda and the Milky Way. Also, uneven gravitational attraction on some galaxies, due to the mass of surrounding galaxies, might have caused them to start to rotate which, eventually, might have flattened them into discs. Both Andromeda and the Milky Way have the general form of rotating discs.

## Where did the stars come from?

Within individual galaxies, matter then became more and more concentrated by gravitational attraction, into even more localized clumps, which were to become individual stars. As more and more matter accumulated (remember that we are still talking of a time when only hydrogen, helium and a small quantity of lithium existed), the cores of many of these proto-stars became extremely dense; very much denser than any material we know on Earth.

In addition, as extra material was attracted to the forming star by gravity, the gravitational field would accelerate it and, when it hit the core of the star, the collision might be quite violent. As the atoms were forced together in collisions in these very dense cores, the temperature rose further. Eventually, the temperature became so high, perhaps 10 million degrees, that nuclear fusion was able to restart.

We previously encountered nuclear fusion reactions in the early universe, but those only lasted for a brief spell of a few minutes. The fusion reactions in the heart of a star can continue for billions of years.

That is the process that is happening in The Sun as you read this. It has been going on for the last 4.5 billion years or so. For all that time, The Sun has been converting something like 600 million tons of hydrogen into helium every second and, in the process, about four million tons of material is converted into energy every second. That is the source of all The Sun's heat and light, only a tiny fraction of which reaches Earth. The Sun is so massive that it is expected to keep this up for about another five billion years.

For other stars, the timescales differ from those of The Sun, depending on their masses, but the process is the same. Therefore, in all the galaxies, local concentrations of matter became so dense that they could ignite themselves as stars. The universe once again had light sources within it, after an absence of a few hundred million years since the microwave background radiation had been emitted.

The next two sections contain a bit more information about the evolution of stars. The important point for now is that all of the heavier elements than lithium are produced in stars, together with some more helium and lithium, extra to that which was originally formed in the big bang itself. All the oxygen, carbon, nitrogen, calcium and phosphorus, which make up about 99 percent of your body (along with hydrogen from the big bang), and the other elements that make up the rest, were manufactured in stars. Therefore, to the best of our scientific knowledge, we humans actually are stardust.

How did these chemical elements get from stars into you? In the next section, we shall see that stars have a finite life, because they eventually use up all their fuel. Stars that are somewhat more massive than The Sun then end their lives in gigantic explosions called supernovae, which blow off the outer layers of the stars into space. The chemical elements that the stars have manufactured therefore end up as clouds of gas and dust in space.[45]

Gravitational attraction between particles of dust in the ejected clouds of material can then cause them to start to come together again. The more mass that comes together, the greater is its gravitational effect on any surrounding gas and dust. In this way, a new generation of stars is formed. The types of stars which end their lives in explosions have much shorter lives than The Sun, so there has been time for more than one generation of stars to form, which is why our Sun is 'only' about 4.5 billion years old, and why it formed with elements able to give it some rocky planets including, of course, Earth.

You are made, indirectly, from chemicals available on Earth, so the stuff from which you are made is therefore billions of years old, and has had an interesting life in the extreme pressure and heat of the nuclear reactor at the center of a long-dead star, and then in the extreme cold (almost -273°C) of outer space.

## How many stars?

How big is the visible universe, in terms of the number of stars it contains? If you are religious this amounts to asking how extensive is the part of God's creation we can see; there is still very much more that we cannot see.

In excellent viewing conditions, we can observe perhaps five or six thousand points of light in the night sky, with the naked eye. Pre-twentieth-century scientists were correct in thinking that almost all of these were stars, similar to our Sun, which are all in our own galaxy, the Milky Way. What they did not know, however, is that the Milky Way contains at least 200 billion stars.[46] That is an enormous number which is hard to visualize but, undaunted, we shall try shortly.

The distances involved are also extremely large. The Andromeda galaxy, the only large galaxy in the 'neighborhood' of the Milky Way, is about 2.5 million light years away. The Milky Way is about 100,000 light years in diameter, so it would take 25 Milky Way galaxies, side by side, to span the distance to Andromeda.

With the aid of telescopes, huge numbers of other galaxies become visible. It is now thought that there are at least 100 billion galaxies in the visible universe, each containing an average of perhaps 100 billion stars.

Now we enter the realms of very silly numbers! If there are 100 billion galaxies, each with 100 billion stars on average, then the total number of stars in the visible universe is 100 billion times 100 billion. That is 10 thousand billion billion. Such a number probably seems completely meaningless. As with the initial temperature of the universe in the big bang, discussed earlier, any other way of writing such a number will be equally meaningless. For example, it is ten billion trillion, or one followed by 22 zeros or, in scientific notation, $10^{22}$.

Here is a way in which it might be possible to begin to appreciate just how huge this number of stars really is. Try tipping some grains of table salt into the palm of your hand, and counting them. The number of grains might be quite large, even for a modest quantity of salt.

Since there are many varieties of salt, some much coarser than others, for the illustrations in the following paragraphs to work, we need to define a standard salt grain! For our purposes, it is a perfect cube, with each side half a millimeter long. You could therefore line up twenty such grains against a one centimeter division on a rule, and eight such grains can be packed into one cubic millimeter – four arranged into a 1mm square, half a millimeter thick, on top of another four arranged into a 1mm square, half a millimeter thick.

Now imagine something the size of an eating apple, slightly smaller than a tennis ball, packed with as many salt grains as it is possible to arrange inside it. Try to imagine the size of the pile of grains if you were to tip them all onto a table to try to count them. In fact, there would be about one million[47] and, if you could count them at four grains per second (about the fastest it is possible to count small coins off the edge of a table), it would take you almost three days. One million is a negligibly small number though, compared with the number of stars in the universe.

As an intermediate step, let's think about the 200 billion stars (at least) in the Milky Way. One cubic meter has 1,000 mm along each edge, so its volume is one billion cubic millimeters – that's eight billion of our salt grains. Therefore we need 25 cubic meters of salt grains just to represent the number of stars in our own galaxy. That's the size of a room, 4 meters long, 2.5 meters wide and 2.5 meters high, full of salt grains. Counting the 200 billion salt grains which it would take to fill that room, at four per second, never pausing for anything, would take over 1,584 years.[48] To finish counting in 2014, you would have had to have begun in the year 430, the year in which St. Augustine died; and no stopping, remember!

Now that is still only the number of stars in our galaxy and, since there are at least 100 billion galaxies, we are still not even scratching the surface. We still need a much larger salt-holder. So imagine a large, world-class stadium, such as the 90,000-seat Wembley stadium in

London (as reopened in 2007). Try to imagine, if you can, that stadium completely full to the top with salt grains.

According to several web sites, the Wembley stadium has a volume of 1,139,100 cubic meters. Wembley would therefore hold about $9.11 \times 10^{15}$ salt grains (9.11 million billion). At the usual counting rate of four grains per second, 24 hours per day, it would now take about 72 million years to count those salt grains. Humans have only walked the Earth for perhaps 200,000 years, so that is about 360 times the time for which humans have existed. However, that is the time to count 'only' one Wembley-full of salt.

This number of salt grains is still a hopelessly insignificant fraction of the number required to represent the $10^{22}$ stars in the universe, but we are nearly there as far as this thought experiment goes.

Remember the apple, whose space would contain one million grains, which you would struggle to count in three days? Well, if you replace each individual one of those one million salt grains with a complete Wembley stadium full of salt (so now you have one million Wembleys full of salt grains), that is roughly $10^{22}$ salt grains, the same as the number of stars in the visible universe. Counting those at 4 per second would take nearly 6,000 times as long as the 13.7 billion year age of the universe itself.

Your mind may be reeling, but this may have given you some idea of just how enormous is the number of stars in our galaxy (the number of grains of salt in a room 4m×2.5m×2.5m), and how utterly unimaginable is the number of stars in the entire universe (the number of grains of salt in one million Wembley stadiums, with one million being represented by the number of salt grains which would fill an apple).

People sometimes ask why God would need to create so many stars, if we are the only civilization in the universe. Well, who says we are? However, setting that aside for now, there are good reasons why there are huge numbers of stars, and why the universe needs to be so old. We shall come back to these things later.

## The lives of the stars

In the life of the universe, one of the more remarkable chains of coincidences is the one that is necessary in order for carbon to be able to exist at all. Given that all life on Earth is carbon-based, we are only here as the result of that chain of coincidences. Since it occurs in stars, we need to look into the life of stars, at least a little, in order to be able to appreciate it.

There are four fundamental forces in nature, and they play an important part in what follows. The first two fundamental forces are everyday ones with which we are familiar. The first is the force of gravity.[49] It is gravity that attracts your book towards Earth, and hence pulls it down onto your desk.

The second everyday force is the electromagnetic force, which results in attraction between opposite electrical charges, or opposite magnetic poles; and repulsion between similar electrical charges, or similar magnetic poles.[50] This is the force that prevents your book from passing through your desk! Let me explain.

Your desk is made of atoms and, as we have already mentioned, atoms are mainly empty space. The amount of empty space in an atom varies a lot depending on the chemical element involved, but it is not untypical for the diameter of an atom to be 100,000 times the diameter of its nucleus. If you imagine Earth as being an atom, its nucleus, at the center, might be only 120 meters in diameter; the rest would be almost entirely empty space.

These relatively enormous spaces between the atomic nuclei in your desk are occupied only by the tiny, orbiting electrons. It is the electromagnetic attraction between the (negatively-charged) outer electrons of one atom and the (positively-charged) protons in the nucleus of an adjacent one, which binds them together into molecules, and then into solid materials – though those 'solid' materials do remain, mostly, empty space. This is illustrated by the fact that a small sub-atomic particle such as a neutrino can pass straight through Earth without hitting anything.

The other two fundamental forces are less familiar, as they operate only at the sub-atomic scale. The strong nuclear force binds atomic nuclei together. It is a short-range force which overcomes the electromagnetic repulsion between protons if they can get closer to each other than about one trillionth ($10^{-12}$) of a millimeter. The weak nuclear force is even shorter range, and is responsible for conversions between the smallest sub-atomic particles of matter. It acts only over about one thousandth of the scale of the strong nuclear force, so over much smaller distances even than the sizes of protons and neutrons. It is responsible, for example, for the decay of radioactive Carbon-14, mentioned in an earlier endnote.[51]

Stars spend much of their lives converting hydrogen to helium by nuclear fusion, and releasing lots of energy as heat and light in the process. The details of the fusion reactions in stars differ from those in the big bang because there were no free neutrons left over from the big bang, since neutrons decay into more fundamental particles after a while – unless they are part of a stable atom.[51]

Instead, because the core of a star is so hot, hydrogen nuclei (protons) can move with enough speed so that, if they collide, they have sufficient energy to temporarily overcome the electromagnetic force of repulsion arising from their positive charges. That means that protons can get close enough for the strong nuclear force to bind them together into a helium nucleus.

A helium nucleus needs two protons and two neutrons though, so what actually happens is that four protons come together, two of them having been converted into neutrons. That conversion process is one of the things for which the weak nuclear force is responsible. Davies[30] points out that it is fortunate that the weak force actually is so weak, because this slows down the rate of hydrogen conversion in stars, and thus allows them to shine for sufficient billions of years for a planet such as Earth to become capable of supporting life.

The long-term fate of a star depends upon its mass. During the hydrogen conversion phase, which can last for billions of years, a normal star is kept stable because the outward pressure from the nuclear reactions at its core, balances the shrinking of the star due to the inward pull of gravity. Once sufficient of the hydrogen has been used up in producing helium, the outward pressure due to nuclear fusion decreases and the star begins to collapse under the influence of its own gravity. The core of the star therefore becomes denser. How long this takes, and what happens next, depends on the mass of the star. More massive stars generate higher internal pressures and temperatures, and therefore use their fuel faster, resulting in shorter lives than less massive stars.[52]

## How was the carbon for life formed?

Stars of between about one half, and three times, the mass of The Sun, after converting a lot of their hydrogen into helium, and undergoing gravitational contraction, become hot enough and dense enough for further nuclear reactions to occur. To manufacture carbon by nucleosynthesis requires a core temperature of 100 million degrees or more.

The Sun is presently in the earlier phase of its life, largely converting hydrogen to helium, and its core temperature is about 16 million degrees. However, over billions of years, this will increase as the hydrogen fuel becomes depleted and The Sun begins to collapse and become denser. That is the stage of a star's life at which the previously mentioned coincidences are necessary for the formation of carbon.

A normal carbon atom has six protons and six neutrons in its nucleus.[38] In contrast, the lighter helium atom has two protons and two neutrons. Therefore, it was initially thought that carbon might be made by the direct fusion of three helium nuclei. However, the dynamics of that reaction are not sufficiently rapid to explain the formation of carbon in stars, because the chances of three helium nuclei colliding in a manner that would bind them all together into a carbon nucleus are exceedingly small.

A more plausible explanation, requiring only collisions between two suitable particles, rather than three, is that two helium nuclei would be fused to create a nucleus of beryllium-8, with four protons and four neutrons.[53] A further helium nucleus would then be fused with the beryllium nucleus to create a carbon nucleus.

Interestingly, the beryllium-8 nucleus is unstable. It decays back to helium within about $10^{-16}$ second of being formed; that's a ten-thousandth of a trillionth of a second. The chances of making many carbon atoms in that sort of timescale are still extremely slim.

The astronomer and mathematician Fred Hoyle, born in God's own county of Yorkshire, was amongst the pioneers of identifying the nuclear reactions within stars. In 1954, he thought about this problem from an anthropic point of view. To look at the universe anthropically is, at its simplest, to argue that because we are here to investigate the universe, then the universe must have evolved in whatever way was necessary to lead to the presence of humans, however unlikely that may seem.

Hoyle argued that since he contained a lot of carbon, and since carbon is produced in stars, it was impossible that the short lifetime of beryllium 8 could halt the sequence of nucleosynthesis in stars, because stars must have produced an awful lot more carbon than was suggested by the brief opportunities afforded by the lifetime of the beryllium-8 nucleus.

After thinking about the problem, Hoyle concluded that there must be a so-called 'resonance' in the carbon atom, which would make the production of carbon by fusion between beryllium and helium much more efficient. That, in turn, would mean that less time would be required to complete the reaction, and that many more carbon nuclei could therefore be formed during the short lifetimes of beryllium-8 nuclei.

I have often demonstrated large-scale resonance to my students by standing on a desk and swinging a pendulum, made of a mass of about half a kilogram on the end of a meter and a half of string. If you try this (you know you want to) you will find that by varying the frequency of oscillation of the pendulum (by moving your hand from side to side at different rates), one specific frequency can be found at which the size of the pendulum's oscillation is many times greater than the size of the oscillation of your hand. That's 'resonance' in this sense; if you either speed up the oscillation of your hand, or slow it down, the size of the pendulum's oscillation will dramatically decrease, relative to that of your hand, compared with what it was in the previously-described resonant condition.

In the resonant condition, the pendulum can be kept swinging at a large amplitude with a minimum of energy input. The resonance in nuclear reactions is a similar phenomenon – it is a particular energy level at which the reaction proceeds much more rapidly than it would if the energy of the reacting particles was either slightly higher or slightly lower.

Hoyle calculated the energy level at which the resonance would need to occur in the carbon nucleus, in order to allow stars to produce sufficient carbon to account for the proportion of carbon we now see around the universe. He asked his physicist colleagues whether there was such a resonance, but they told him that there was not.

Hoyle, however, remained convinced that his suggestion was the only solution to the problem of the existence of carbon in the quantities we observe, so he persuaded a physicist friend of his to search for such a resonance. It was soon discovered, at exactly the energy level that Hoyle had predicted, much to the physicists' surprise. There is a quotation somewhere indicating that the physicists were amazed that Hoyle could make correct predictions about the details of atomic physics, which was not his subject, simply by thinking about stars. It is this kind of consistency and reliability in science which persuades some scientists that there is a rational Mind behind the laws of nature which we discover.

That was an excellent indicator that Hoyle's theories of nuclear fusion were correct. It does mean, though, that our existence is highly improbable. Were it not for that resonance, at exactly the required energy level in the carbon atom, there would be insufficient carbon in the universe for life, as we know it, to be able to exist.[54]

That's not the end of the story though. It is also the case that, if another helium nucleus then fused with a carbon nucleus, an oxygen nucleus would result. It turns out that there is also a resonance in the oxygen atom that could allow this to happen so easily that all the carbon would then be converted to oxygen – which, again, would mean that we would not be here to discuss it. However, this resonance is at an energy level slightly too low for this to be the case. As a result, this chain of reactions stops at carbon, whilst oxygen is manufactured in different reactions later.

If the resonance in the carbon atom was absent, or at a slightly different energy level (perhaps only 3% lower), then there would be no carbon in the universe, and hence no life as we know it. If the resonant energy level in the oxygen atom had been just 1% higher, all the carbon would have been converted to oxygen and, again, there would be no carbon and no life.

Also, recall from the previous section that we are only here to talk about this double coincidence because of an additional coincidence – namely that the weak nuclear force is sufficiently weak to allow The Sun to burn for long enough for all this to happen at all. We return to these types of multiple coincidences later.

Stars more than about three times as massive as The Sun, go on to generate all the elements from carbon through to iron, by various nucleosynthesis reactions.[55] The process stops at iron, which has 26 protons and 30 neutrons in its nucleus, because iron has the most stable atomic structure of any element, and will not take part in further nucleosynthesis reactions. Large stars therefore accumulate massive iron cores. However, if that was the end of the story, there would be no elements heavier than iron.

In terms of mass, iron is only the 56th element out of the 118 that we know, so there is clearly some other mechanism, yet to be explained, by which the others can be created. Many of the elements heavier than uranium don't exist naturally on Earth. We can only make them in nuclear reactors, or fleetingly in high-energy particle accelerators. But there are certainly plenty of well-known elements with heavier atoms than iron, including copper, zinc, silver, tin, xenon, tungsten, gold, mercury, lead, uranium and plutonium.

In very massive stars, gravitational collapse at the ends of their lives can result in the sudden fusing of their iron cores. This happens when the iron core has become so massive that it can no longer support its own weight, so the empty space within its atoms suddenly collapses. This can happen in just a second or two, and may release more energy in one second than our Sun will release in its entire lifetime.[56] The resulting explosion, known as a supernova, may be as bright as 10 billion Suns. The elements heavier than iron are manufactured in these explosions, which also eject all the elements made by the star into space.

Stars that end their lives in supernovae use their fuel relatively quickly compared with The Sun, perhaps in just a few million years. There has been plenty of time for massive second and third generation stars, which incorporate the heavier elements manufactured by earlier stars, to form the elements higher up the periodic table than iron. Thus, as we noted earlier, all the naturally occurring chemical elements are eventually manufactured inside stars, and are made available for use elsewhere by exploding stars.

In the next chapter we shall end these predominantly scientific discussions with a look at the evolution of life on Earth. Then we shall take a straightforward, but possibly surprising, look at how the story of creation, as told in these chapters, relates to the one told in the Bible.

## Chapter 6  The Evolution of Life

Since Charles Darwin's time, there have been disagreements between some scientists and some religious people, particularly more fundamentalist Christians, about the extent of the evolution of living things. In the case of Christianity, the first two chapters of the Bible (in the book of Genesis) seem to suggest that God created all the plants and animals directly, including humans, in six days. Some religious people, who want to understand those six days of Genesis literally, believe that the plants and animals were created more-or-less as we see them now.

On the other hand, since the mid nineteenth century, science has provided a different scenario. This is based on our knowledge of heredity stemming from the work of Gregor Mendel (published in 1866), Darwin's theory of evolution by natural selection (published in 1859), and the study of fossils. However, agreement within the scientific community, about the extent to which evolutionary ideas apply, is currently not as strong as, say, the agreement over the big bang theory of creation.

Few scientifically aware people would seriously suggest that evolution doesn't take place at all; there is plenty of evidence indicating that it does. Often-quoted examples include the mutation of influenza viruses, and 'super-bugs' in hospitals, as they evolve to survive the latest generation of treatment; or the color of moth's wings evolving to match the lightening of tree bark, where the smoke of a former industrial zone has been replaced with much cleaner air; or the improvements in humans' natural resistance to malaria, in countries where malaria is endemic.

Science's explanation begins with the study of heredity – the way in which plants and animals inherit characteristics from their parents, via genes encoded within the DNA molecule,[57] about which we shall say more shortly.

It seems obvious that we inherit characteristics from our parents. Less obviously, we now understand that small random mutations can occur in genes during the process of passing on those characteristics from parents to descendants. Darwin's theory of evolution by natural selection, then explains that any advantageous mutations are more likely to be passed on to the next generation, whilst unsuccessful mutations are less likely to be passed on.

Here's an example to clarify the ideas behind this theory, which is known as Neo-Darwinism. Imagine that two animals mate, but that a small random error occurs in the copying of genetic information during the process of conception. As a result, their offspring is born with a mutated gene that neither of its parents had. Let's say that this mutation has caused a slight change to its eyes, in a way which allows it to see a little better than its parents could.

More importantly, it can also see a little better than its contemporaries can, so perhaps it will be a little better at finding food than they are, and a little better at avoiding predators than they are. That will make it a little more likely to survive long enough to mate, and thus to pass on that modification for slightly better sight to the next generation.

Its offspring will, in turn, out-compete their contemporaries, and pass on the beneficial mutation when they mate with those contemporaries. In this way, the beneficial modification will gradually spread throughout the population, as those with the competitive edge of slightly better sight gradually replace those with the old, slightly inferior sight.

In some future generation, another mutation during conception may cause a further slight improvement in the ability to see, and so the process continues, improving the sight of the population as a whole as time passes. This process is what we believe to be happening with regard to malaria resistance in some human populations.

On the other hand, an unfavorable genetic mutation that, for example, causes a reduction in the ability to see well, will have the opposite effect. The offspring may be less successful at finding food and avoiding predators, and therefore less likely to survive long enough to pass on that unsuccessful genetic mutation to the next generation; so bad mutations tend to be suppressed.

In this way, animals evolve, little by little as the generations go by, to be more successful. The same applies to plants, in which minor random genetic mutations might lead to a slightly better, or worse, chance of getting pollinated.

It is important to note that a 'successful' mutation is only one that makes it more likely that an animal or plant will live long enough to produce offspring. From a purely evolutionary viewpoint, once an organism has passed on its genes to the next generation, its job is done. Anything in its genetic makeup, which helps it to live on for a long time after breeding age, is just good fortune.[58]

Such scientific ideas do not sit well with some of the religious views at first sight. The extreme version of the scientific description, in theory at least, only needs one pair of primitive living organisms of some kind, or perhaps even just one, and everything else can then develop from that by means of heredity and natural selection.

For an all-encompassing scientific description, the main problem is to explain how the first life arose, since before that there were, by definition, only inanimate (non-living) chemicals. We do not seem to be anywhere near to understanding that. Darwin's theory is about the origin of species in existing living things, not the origin of life itself.

Another problem, which is still the subject of serious scientific debate, is whether there are some things that are too complex to have been able to evolve, either at all, or within the time span that has been available.

When I first seriously considered the claims of Christianity on my life, the differences between the literal 'six-day' view and the evolutionary view were a problem for me. But I then discovered that there are different, perfectly valid interpretations of Genesis, which allow the scientific and biblical accounts of creation to co-exist happily. Some of those will be mentioned in the next chapter.

On the scientific side, there are some, such as Richard Dawkins, who firmly believe that evolution can completely explain the entire history of the development of life on Earth, and that science will solve the problem of the origin of life. There are others, such as Michael Behe, who are unconvinced. In some cases, they think that there has been insufficient time for all the required incremental developments to occur, in others they believe that some items are just too complex to have evolved by a series of small, incremental changes. Behe, for example, also discusses the results of analyzing many thousands of successive generations of bacteria that, he says, indicate that, "It is easier for evolution to break things than to make things."

That quotation from Behe comes from John Lennox's book *God's Undertaker*.[59] The popular writings and broadcasts of Richard Dawkins might suggest to the casual observer that the all-encompassing version of evolution is a done deal. However, Lennox shows that there is also a serious body of opinion, based on evidence from experiments in genetics and heredity, which questions, "Whether the evolutionary mechanism can bear all the weight that is put upon it."

Whatever may be the relative technical merits of these views, any scientific studies of the origin of life, or of evolution, are attempting to answer the 'how' questions – *how* did life arise, and *how* did we get here as a result? There is also a personal explanation for these things (see Chapter One), in terms of the 'why' questions – *why* did life arise, and *why* are we here?

If the answers to those 'why' questions lie in purposes in the Mind of God, it then follows that, whatever the scientists eventually agree 'evolution' to be, it is God's chosen method of building a world full of life. We can therefore enjoy being fascinated by the details of *how* it might all have come about, in terms of the mechanisms and processes described by science, without any threat to our religious faith in God, whose idea it was.

Amongst those arguing in these areas are evolutionists, anti-evolutionists, 'old-Earth' and 'young-Earth' creationists, members of the Intelligent Design movement (see later) and others, all holding different views. It is worthwhile discussing the differences, but they are not of lasting significance compared with the question of whether God wants to have a relationship with us, for example.

There is an obvious temptation here for religious folk to invoke a 'god of the gaps'. For example, perhaps God created life, and then science describes how it evolved afterwards. Those who tend to that kind of view must be careful of relying too much on such a proposal. Although it isn't looking particularly likely, science may eventually fill that gap by discovering a mechanism for the origin of life from inanimate chemicals; there have been various suggestions, but they have been too speculative to find wide acceptance to date. We just don't know.

As usual though, even if science does find the mechanism, it will not investigate any reason as to *why* it happened, in the sense of a potential purpose behind it, because, as we have seen, science doesn't ask that kind of question. Religious people will therefore always be free to claim that it was God's idea, and God's chosen mechanism of putting the idea into practice; whereas an atheistic scientist can only say, "There is no purpose, it just happened like that, and that's all there is to it." For anyone with that kind of viewpoint, the description of the universe must always remain incomplete.

Perhaps a more satisfactory way out of this problem, which does not rely on a god of the gaps, is the idea that God, in some sense, allows the universe to make itself (the origin of this idea is described later). In other words, God knew what kind of universe he wanted there to be, and instituted certain processes to allow it to develop in that way. Now he guides and sustains it within limits that he has set.

It turns out that this idea, like most, has been around for ages, but I can still remember the feeling of 'light dawning' when I first read, in the writings of John Polkinghorne[60], that the universe might be allowed to make itself. There are some difficulties with this view, which are mentioned later. For now, it can be summarized as stating that the big bang was God's chosen method of creation, and that evolution, whatever that eventually turns out to mean, is his chosen method of allowing species to develop on Earth.

One related question is whether the future is 'open' to some extent. Does God still influence events, or did he just put his feet up after the big bang and leave everything to its own devices? Assuming that God does have a relationship with people who accept him, and that he therefore listens to their prayers, it would be strange if the world always rolled along, following a pre-set plan, without any potential for those prayers to have an effect. How God's potential actions in the world might tie in with our free will, and with the fact that the universe appears to proceed according to the reliable laws discovered by science, is something else that we shall consider later.

## Cells, genetics and DNA

The previous chapters have mentioned some of the large-scale aspects of creation. Now it is time for a brief look at some of the sub-microscopic biological wonders within all of us.

We know that living things are constructed from cells, which are usually quite small. Human cells vary in size, perhaps by a factor of 10 or so, but many are just one or two hundredths of a millimeter across. However, although cells are so small, there is a lot of molecular machinery packed inside them, so the scale of that molecular machinery, which is very intricate and remarkably elegant in operation, is going to be much smaller still.

Estimates seem to vary a lot here, but there are perhaps $10^{14}$ (100 trillion) cells in your body. Inside each one, there are many distinct arrangements called organelles, each of which performs a specific function inside the cell, much as an organ such as your pancreas or heart performs its function inside your body as a whole. Two of these are the mitochondria (of which there are many in each cell) and the cell nucleus (of which there is one). For the moment, we shall just note that mitochondria convert energy from food into a form that the rest of the cell can use, whilst a cell's nucleus controls much of what the cell does, such as when it should grow, or divide, or die.

You began as a single cell at your conception. That cell then divided into two, then each of those divided, resulting in a total of four cells, then many further divisions of successive generations of cell occurred, eventually resulting in the trillions of cells which you now are. Interestingly, if it was simply a matter of each cell dividing into two, then each of those dividing into two, and so on, it would take only 47 steps of cell division to get from a single cell to 100 trillion.

In order for a cell to be able to divide into two, it must be able to self-replicate. In other words, it effectively needs to be able to manufacture a copy of itself. One of the defining characteristics of a living thing is that it can self-replicate (OK, it might often take two living things, but one is enough at the scale of cells).

Some popular-science books and television programs point out that amino acids, which are some of the basic building blocks of living things, can be created spontaneously in various ways. That's fair enough. However, they then go on to assume that the fact that amino acids can potentially form in a number of environments, means that it is very likely that there is life in many other places in the universe. That may, or may not, be correct, but it does not follow from the argument about amino acids. Amino acids remain inanimate chemicals, and we still don't have much of a clue as to how the first self-replicating cell could have arisen from those.

Whatever view you take of the improbable first appearance of self-replicating cells, life does depend upon them. Each cell contains the molecular machinery that can carry out self-replication. However, there is even more to it than that. Different organs in our bodies contain different types of cell; red blood cells are different from heart muscle cells, which are different from liver cells, for example.

The same applies to the different parts of all other animals and plants, except for some primitive organisms with few cells. There is therefore the additional problem that, when a cell is about to divide to replicate, it must somehow 'know' what type of cell is required next.

The DNA molecule carries the instructions for cell division, growth and death. Most DNA is contained in the cell nucleus, but there is also a small ring of DNA in each of the thousands of mitochondria in every cell. All of it is capable of replication. Cells also contain many other complex sub-systems which we haven't even mentioned, and which contain no DNA. Although DNA molecules vary in size, and can be quite large by molecular standards, they are clearly therefore very small indeed by the standards of everyday objects.

I am unqualified to discuss molecular biology in any detail beyond a general scientific awareness, but I do want to provide just a brief glimpse as to how intricate and elegant DNA and its workings are, as an indication of why there are things whose origins we are still struggling to understand.

As usual, I am not relying on the suggestion that God must therefore have directly organized these things – though he might have done; rather, I am trying to pass on a little of my own sense of wonder at such things, and the awe with which I regard the Mind behind it all.

You might disagree that there is such a "Mind behind it all", but there are also many scientists who would disagree that what is described below is likely to have come about entirely by chance, even given billions of years of gradual selective evolution.

My feelings of awe at the structure and workings of DNA, and my sympathy towards the notion that they hint at a creative Designer, do not arise from any naivety on my part. I am, in fact, in extremely well informed company here. For example, two highly regarded Christian authors, whose work I refer to below, are Alister McGrath and Francis Collins. McGrath is now a well-known theologian, but originally obtained his PhD in molecular biophysics; Collins, for 10 years, headed up the international project responsible for decoding the human genome, and stood beside President Bush when the completion of the project was announced. At the time of writing, Collins was the Director of the National Institutes of Health in the USA, one of the world's foremost scientific posts. It is interesting that both McGrath and Collins were self-confessed atheists, before becoming Christians.

There follows some brief detail of the overall structure of DNA and how it is arranged into chromosomes. For further details, consult books such as those of Collins and McGrath referenced in these endnotes. [61] [62] The website of the prestigious journal *Nature* was also very informative in this kind of area at the time of writing.[63]

The form of the DNA molecule is a double helix. To visualize its structure, imagine taking a long, narrow, flexible ladder, fixing one end to something rigid, and then twisting the free end of the ladder through 360° a number of times, like winding up a clockwork toy. Alternatively, think of a long 'spiral' staircase.

McGrath points out that, in the DNA molecule, the 'rungs' of the 'ladder' are approximately two nanometers wide. That is two millionths of a millimeter, or $2 \times 10^{-9}$ meter, perhaps one ten-thousandth of the thickness of a human hair. Even using the most powerful optical microscopes, it is impossible to see something as narrow as that, because the wavelength of visible light is too long.

The sidepieces of the DNA ladder are made of phosphates and sugars, but the rungs are much more interesting. The number of rungs in the ladder, and hence the length of the molecule, depends upon what kind of organism the DNA belongs to, and what the specific purpose of the DNA is. According to McGrath, the spacing between each pair of rungs in the ladder is about 0.34 nanometers ($3.4 \times 10^{-10}$ meter), and each twist of the double helix takes place over about 10 rungs.

Each rung is made up of exactly two different molecules, known as 'bases', and each rung of the ladder is therefore known as a 'base pair'. The length of a DNA molecule is specified in terms of the number of base pairs it contains, which is the same as specifying the length of a ladder by the number of rungs it has. Some DNA can be less than 100 base pairs long, whereas some human DNA has hundreds of thousands of base pairs.

There are only four base molecules in DNA: adenine, cytosine, guanine and thymine, universally referred to as A, C, G and T. Because of their chemical structures, A and T always appear together as one rung, and C and G always appear together as one rung.

DNA is organized into chromosomes, which are small cores of protein with lengths of DNA packed around them. The DNA carrying the three billion base pairs of the human genome is divided between 24 chromosomes. The nucleus of almost every human cell contains 46 chromosomes, made up of two copies of the chromosomes imaginatively known as '1' to '22' (one copy from the mother and one from the father), plus two 'X' chromosomes in a female, or one 'X' and one 'Y' chromosome in a male.

If the DNA in all 46 chromosomes were to be joined together in a single DNA molecule, it would be getting on for two meters long. The *Nature* web site[63] gives a calculation showing that, if all the DNA in your body were to be uncoiled and joined together, it would stretch around Earth's equator two and a half million times, or to The Sun and back more than 300 times.

A cell might be just one or two hundredths of a millimeter across, and its nucleus is just one small internal part of it. Therefore, in order to fit roughly two meters of DNA into the nucleus of each one of your trillions of cells, the proteins, which form the cores of the chromosomes, have to be very good at compacting the DNA ladders. Protein molecules carry out many such organizational tasks within cells, and Collins points out that some can act like scissors and some like glue, for example.

Now we turn to heredity and genes, to see a little of what DNA does in practice. To set the scene, here is an abbreviated series of historical events, loosely based on Alister McGrath's presentation of them.

In the mid nineteenth century, the monk Gregor Mendel experimented extensively whilst growing pea plants in the garden of his monastery. Over many thousands of trials, he carefully recorded how characteristics such as the colors of the flowers were passed from one generation to succeeding generations. As a result, he realized that he was seeing definite patterns emerging, and he was able to formulate some statistical rules describing the inheritance of characteristics by successive generations.

Mendel also realized that the information governing inheritance of characteristics must be being passed from one generation to the next in discrete packages, in order to account for the numerical rules that he had discovered.

In the early twentieth century, Thomas Hunt Morgan took up Mendel's ideas and carried out extensive experiments in breeding fruit flies. He also observed the transmission of various characteristics from one generation to later generations; in this case it was characteristics such as the colors of the flies' eyes.

Scientists had, by then, discovered that chromosomes appeared when cells divided, and Morgan was able to show that it was these which were responsible for passing on information governing the inheritance of characteristics. His fruit flies had four large chromosomes, and Morgan discovered that there were four sets of traits which appeared to be inherited together in the fruit flies, and that these sets of traits were linked to the four chromosomes. This was an important step towards identifying the discrete packages of inheritance suggested by Mendel.

At that time, however, nobody really knew what the chromosomes were. The structure of DNA had not yet been discovered, and although Morgan could see the relatively large chromosomes under his microscope, he could not see the DNA because it is too narrow. We now know that sections of DNA, located on the chromosomes, contain this hereditary information, and we call Mendel's unit of heredity the gene.

The ladder of the DNA molecule therefore contains some collections of rungs (base pairs) that are our genes. Genes vary in extent. Some can occupy hundreds of rungs of the DNA molecule, others many thousands (Collins). The human genome contains about 25,000 genes, distributed between the 24 different types of chromosome.

We are gradually beginning to unravel where specific genes, responsible for specific things, are located within the human genome. For example, Collins describes the search for the gene responsible for cystic fibrosis. In 1985 it was narrowed down to, "Somewhere within a two million base-pair segment of DNA on chromosome 7."[61] He goes on to say that, in 1989, it was discovered that just three letters in a previously unknown gene were responsible in most cases. The "letters" here are the A, C, G or T of the DNA rungs, and we shall see, shortly, why the "three" is significant.

Early workers in the field of heredity and cell biology didn't believe that the DNA material in the cell nucleus could be responsible for controlling inheritance or the development of the human body. It seemed too simple to contain that kind of information, because each rung could be only one of four possibilities (A-T, C-G, G-C or T-A). They thought that protein molecules must somehow be responsible, since they appeared to be more complex.

They were only partly right, in the sense that it is proteins that determine the color of our eyes, and a host of other things about us; but overall they were wrong, because those proteins, which constitute much of our bodies and control the way we work, are actually manufactured by complex molecular machines inside cells, according to instructions carried by the cell's DNA. So it is our DNA that is actually responsible for inherited characteristics.

As a further example of something that can fill us with awe, consider the following brief summaries of just one or two aspects of how DNA works. As you read this, think about the difficulties that the biologists face in trying to work out how these processes might perhaps have evolved through many gradual small steps.

Despite the fact that each rung of the DNA ladder contains one of only four possible base pairs, there are some clever things that arise from the arrangement of the three billion rungs. The key to this is that is it the *sequence* of the base pairs, which form the code making up

DNA's instruction book – the "language of God", as Francis Collins calls it. The number of possible sequences that can be constructed is amazingly large.

If a very short piece of DNA contained only a single base pair, then there would be just the four possibilities as to what that might be: either A-T, C-G, G-C or T-A. If the strand of DNA had a sequence of just two base pairs, the number of possible sequences represented by the two rungs jumps to sixteen. The number of possible sequences increases extremely rapidly as more rungs are added, because it is equal to the four possibilities, raised to the power of the number of rungs.

For a sequence with only 100 base pairs there are about $16 \times 10^{59}$ (from $4^{100}$) possible sequences. Or, if you prefer the long version, 1.6 trillion trillion trillion trillion trillion, the largest number we've seen in this book so far. Compared with such a quantity, even the $10^{22}$ stars in the universe (remember the million Wembleys full of salt grains) are totally insignificant. Even the number of salt grains required to fill the entire volume of Earth a million times over would be totally insignificant. For a DNA molecule with hundreds of thousands of base pairs, the mind boggles!

Clearly, although there are only four different bases, codes of any level of complexity can be constructed from them, based purely on their sequence as rungs in a long ladder of DNA.

In summary, the human genome contains something like 25,000 genes, distributed amongst the three billion DNA base pairs, and arranged on the 46 chromosomes. Each gene is a section of DNA that contains instructions for building proteins. Taken as a whole, they contain the instructions for building you or me, and those instructions are carried inside the nucleus of almost every one of the 100 trillion cells of our bodies.

The execution of the program stored in the sequence of base pairs within a gene (in other words, the carrying out of its instructions) starts with 'messenger RNA' (mRNA). RNA is ribonucleic acid. It contains three of the same bases as DNA (A, C and G), but thymine (T) is replaced by uracil (U). A strand of mRNA carries a copy of the information from one half of a section of DNA, which has been split down the middle.[64]

The mRNA moves out of the cell's nucleus and carries the gene's instructions into the ribosome, which is another organelle within the cell. There, the protein for which the particular gene codes is manufactured. A "team of sophisticated translators" (Collins' words) reads the bases of the mRNA, and each group of three bases (corresponding to three half-rungs from the gene in the original DNA molecule) gives rise to the formation of one of twenty amino acids.

The sequence of amino acids produced from the information in the mRNA then gives rise to the required protein.[65] It is proteins that carry out most tasks within the cell. They also provide its structure (known as a cytoskeleton), and help to pass messages from the outside to the inside of the cell. Some are also exported out of the cell to perform functions elsewhere, such as acting as enzymes to digest food, forming antibodies to resist infection, carrying oxygen around the bloodstream in the form of hemoglobin, forming hair and nails, producing all the muscles and even controlling signaling within the brain.

Looking a little further afield, Collins also points out that the genetic code which gives rise to amino acids, and hence proteins, is the same in all living things. For example, the mRNA three-base sequence GAG codes for the amino acid called glutamic acid, no matter whether it is, "In the language of soil bacteria, the mustard weed, the alligator [or] your aunt Gertrude." (Collins) Incidentally, according to the *Nature* web site so does GAA, as there is some redundancy in this process[65]. A glance through some of the pages of that extensive web site will show that I have barely begun to scratch the surface of the workings of a cell here.

I would not go so far as to say that it is impossible that the mechanisms described above arose by an accumulation of successive small evolutionary changes, starting from inanimate chemicals incapable of replication. But working out how that could happen is a problem that seems nowhere near to being solved.

Maybe these processes did evolve from inanimate chemicals as part of God's evolutionary plan; maybe they were directly instituted by God, in the sense that he might have had some part in directly forming the first life. Either way, the fact that this is just a tiny fraction of what goes on in almost every cell of your body, is another indicator to me (and to some molecular biologists and geneticists such as Alister McGrath and Francis Collins) that the Mind of God is responsible.

This has been only the briefest glimpse of the kind of thing that is going on, at a microscopic scale, inside each of your trillions of cells, as you read this. For an interesting description of additional detail of the internal workings of cells, including the intricate goings-on within the ribosome, try the 'Canterbury' chapter of Richard Dawkins' book *The Ancestor's Tale*.[66]

Since Dawkins is the most prominent of the 'new atheists' you might be surprised that a Christian author would recommend his books. After all, he takes the view that all this clever self-replicating machinery has developed purely by chance, and obviously had nothing whatsoever to do with God (since Dawkins does not believe in God). Scientists such as Collins, McGrath and many others equally obviously disagree with that sentiment entirely.

However, credit where credit is due. When Dawkins writes on biology, he does so extremely well, and his excellent descriptions are well worth reading. It's just a shame that he has the unfortunate habit of losing his objectivity when he writes about God. For example, in his best seller, *The God Delusion*,[67] he did himself no favors by setting up the worst possible caricatures of religion and religious people, so that they were then easy to knock down.

The relevant points here, which Dawkins' book will reinforce, are that the structure of cells is very complex in itself; and that the self-replication of cells, and the building of proteins, both of which are essential for life, are extremely elegant procedures, many of which we understand, but the origin of which we have not yet been able to work out.

## Towards the origin of life?

Anti-evolutionists make much of the gaps in the fossil record. It would be nice to have more of the gaps filled by fossils, but the fact that there are gaps is actually not surprising, given the special set of circumstances which has to exist for a fossil to be formed at all. In addition to the fossil record though, molecular biology has provided us with a lot of DNA analysis that has filled in many of the gaps.

There are now some remarkably detailed diagrams showing the genetic interrelationships of species based on DNA analysis. The Hillis plot, for example, shows the relationships between 3,000 species, though it is impossible to read the detail in a book-sized version. Such diagrams don't tell us about the origin of the first life though. Darwinian evolution only comes into play once some life exists which is capable of evolving into species. Similarly, genetics only comes into play once there are genes that can be passed down to offspring.

It may be that genes, as we now know them, evolved from some simpler coding system. One suggestion has involved certain crystalline silicon structures in primeval mud, for example, but the jury is still out on that type of suggestion, since the leap from non-living to living material remains beyond our current understanding.

There are some widespread misunderstandings of the theory of evolution, which give rise to spurious arguments that would be better avoided. For example, I recall an argument, in print, that evolution cannot be a true theory because plant cells appear in the fossil record before animal cells. That was put forward as being a problem for the theory of evolution, because plant cells contain all the light gathering and photosynthesis machinery, and so they are more complex than animal cells. Evolution must therefore be a mistaken theory, it was said, because more complex things have to come after simpler things.

A biologist would probably reply that there is a false assumption in the question. The later-appearing animal cells did not evolve *from* the photosynthesizing plant cells at all. Rather, both the plant cells and the animal cells developed, in parallel, from some early common ancestor.

Once that common ancestor had given rise to the two offspring whose descendants would gradually diverge to become the plant and animal lines of descent, there would no longer be any evolutionary connection between the complexity of the development of the subsequent plant and animal cells at all. Either of them could have evolved to become the more complex, without any reference to the progress of the other. Also, either of them could have arrived at any given level of complexity before the other.

Some anti-evolutionists also make the more-subtle mistake of arguing that something having the extreme complexity of DNA and its replication mechanisms could not possibly have arisen from inanimate chemicals in a primeval soup. They may be right, but it is dangerous to suggest that it is impossible. It has the feel of another non-argument, based on another misunderstanding.

Even those who dislike the notion of evolution need to understand its fundamentals. Those who do believe it say that it proceeds by small, incremental changes. I don't think any professional molecular biologist or geneticist has suggested that something as complex as DNA could arise, in a single step, from a steamy atmosphere of inanimate chemicals, possibly activated by lightning strikes.[68] Nor would they suggest that the first living organisms were made of cells as advanced as the ones briefly described earlier.

Instead, the evolution of cells and the replicators inside them would be cumulative, working in tiny steps to gradually build the required complexity from simpler forms of life. For example, it is often suggested that RNA, which is much simpler than DNA, may have been the replicator in cells before DNA existed, and it may be possible to visualize how DNA could have evolved from RNA. On that kind of basis, the first form of life would have been much simpler than the type of cell described earlier, and the machinery for replicating it would have had to be much simpler than DNA. Whether or not this is a real possibility, I am unqualified to say.

However, nobody yet has a real solution to the problem of how life, which requires proteins, could exist before the machinery to build those proteins existed. And, of course, the machinery to build those proteins only exists in living systems. Richard Dawkins puts this more accurately in *The Ancestor's Tale*:[66] "A gene big enough to specify an enzyme [a protein necessary for the process of replication] would be too big to replicate accurately without the aid of an enzyme of the very kind that it is trying to specify." He goes on to talk about tentative solutions to this kind of problem but, to the best of my knowledge, none has proved to be generally acceptable.

Dawkins also pointed out many years ago, in *The Blind Watchmaker*,[69] that the arch of a mortar-less stone bridge is built onto scaffolding, or a former. Then, when the arch is finished, with its keystone in place, the former is removed leaving the finished arch standing alone. It is impossible to build the arch one stone at a time, without the former, because the sloping sides would collapse under their own weight before the keystone, which locks it all together, could be installed. In the same kind of way, he suggests, something as complex as DNA would require 'scaffolding' in its evolution.

Dawkins lists two "pillars" of life as DNA and protein, and suggests that scaffolding for holding them in place whilst they evolved side-by-side may have been provided by, perhaps, crystals in clays; and that any record of the scaffolding then vanished, once DNA and proteins were working together in a similar way to that which we see now.

Many of us also have some difficulty in imagining the evolutionary stages of the 3-billion rungs of elegant digital coding, carried by the DNA in the genes of each of our cells. So far as I know, nobody has yet come up with a mechanism as to how that could have arisen from something very much simpler (inanimate, to start with) within the timescale of the existence of life on Earth.

Dawkins' own conclusion about the origin of life, as of his 2009 book *The Greatest Show on Earth*,[70] was that a scheme involving RNA is a likely candidate, because RNA can act like a protein and a replicator in some circumstances.

Even if science does eventually manage to come up with answers to all these questions, those answers are unlikely to displace the belief in a Mind whose idea it all was in the first place. God, as the supreme creative Mind behind the universe, created it in a way which allowed those things to take place in the manner revealed by science. There is therefore no need to be embarrassed if we regard our awe and wonder at creation as another indicator of God's existence. There is more on the relationship of God with his creation, including evolution, in later chapters.

## Intelligent design?

As an introduction to the idea that the world must have had a designer, including a designer of life, the most widely quoted section of text is probably one from William Paley, who was an Anglican clergyman in the eighteenth century. He is famous for his support for natural theology, which studies the universe and what goes on in it, and tries to deduce from such observations the existence of God as its creator. He wrote a number of influential books, one of which was entitled *Natural Theology: Evidences of the Existence and Attributes of the Deity, Collected from the Appearances of Nature*.

The passage in question comes from that book, and is quoted to a greater or lesser extent by many authors. For instance, both Francis Collins and Alister McGrath, whose work has been referenced in the last few pages, quote it. Paley's basic argument goes as follows:

"In crossing a heath, suppose I pitched my foot against a stone, and were asked how the stone came to be there; I might possibly answer that, for anything I knew to the contrary, it had lain there for ever. ... But suppose that I had found a watch upon the ground, and it should be inquired how the watch happened to be in that place. I should hardly think of the answer which I had before given that, for anything I knew, the watch might have always been there. ... The watch must have had a maker ... there must have existed, at some time and at some place or other, an artificer, or artificers who formed it for the purpose which we actually find it to answer, who comprehended its construction and designed its use."

Paley then went on to describe some of the intricate workings of the world, such as the eye, and you can probably guess the inference that he drew from this. The watch is an intricate item, so it must have had an intelligent designer. The workings of the world, especially concerning life, are also intricate, so the world must also have had an intelligent designer.

Many people were convinced by Paley's argument that, wherever we look in the universe, we see things that have the appearance of having been designed by something, or someone, with enormous intelligence. Therefore, they thought, that must be God, and he did indeed design all those things. Many people are still convinced by such arguments today. If we call the intelligent designer God, then this is one part of an 'Argument from Design' for the existence of God.

In Paley's time it was more understandable that people should be convinced by this, but today it requires careful thought, as our knowledge has advanced over the period of more than 200 years since Paley wrote the passage quoted above.

Quite apart from any other consideration, there is a logical flaw in Paley's argument, of which clear thinkers were aware from the start. The fact that two things share one characteristic (complexity, for example) does not mean that they must necessarily share another characteristic (having been designed, for example).

Once you think about it, it is easy to find counter-examples. I have seen a building that is three floors high, but has a long, rectangular, floor-to-roof atrium in the center of it, allowing light from the glass roof to reach the lowest floor. On the upper floors there are railings all the way around this atrium to prevent people falling into it. On each floor, there are rooms all around the atrium, in which people spend their days. The building is a prison, and the inhabitants of the rooms are prisoners.

Many times, I have been into a different building. This building also has a long, rectangular, floor-to-roof atrium in the center to act as a light well. On the upper floors there are railings all the way around the atrium to prevent people falling into it. On each floor, there are rooms all around the atrium, in which people spend their days. So, following Paley's style of reasoning, this building must also be a prison. In fact, it is part of the University at which I spent a large part of my working life; my office was in that particular building for several years. Many people did seem to spend their entire lives there but, as I recall, we were free to leave if we wished.

Let's take a look at Paley's thinking, in the light of more up-to-date knowledge. Since the publication of Darwin's *On the Origin of Species* in 1859, science has suggested that gradual evolution, operating by many small steps over long periods of time, can eventually change living things in fundamental ways, leading to new species. The results of some of those changes, as we now see them, certainly have the appearance of having been deliberately designed for a purpose, but appearances can be deceptive.

It is worth pointing out that there is a distinction between the belief that some aspects of the world point towards the existence of an intelligent designer, and the 'Intelligent Design' (ID) movement.

The former is simply the recognition of clues that point towards the existence of God. The latter (the 'ID movement' with the capital I and capital D) is an organization of people who tend to maintain that an intelligent designer is directly responsible for anything which has the appearance of being too complex to have evolved. In the USA it has also pushed for political change to encourage the teaching of its philosophies in schools in competition with Darwin's theory of natural selection, for example. To me, the ID movement seems too political, and also seems to have some fundamentalist tendencies; if you are interested, you must look into it and make up your own mind!

One thing that the ID movement does is to search for examples of things that are too complex to have evolved. Examples such as the eye have been quoted as being irreducibly complex, and therefore incapable of being produced by a long sequence of small evolutionary changes.[71]

But there are also counter-arguments by evolutionists suggesting quite plausible pathways by which the eye, for example, might have evolved. For instance, it may have begun with a mutation that made a small patch of skin somewhat sensitive to light, which would be useful for evading predators by being able to sense a shadow.

Even Darwin thought that explaining the evolution of the eye might be a problem for his theory. However, not only do we now have explanations as to how the eye might have gradually evolved, but we are also told that it might have evolved on perhaps forty separate occasions.

I don't know enough to adjudicate between the ID movement's search for irreducibly complex examples, and the biologists' suggestions as to how the ID movement might be wrong in each case. But, as always, I am wary of the god of the gaps trap, and my suspicion, based on some of the ingenious explanations I have seen, is that anything which someone describes as being "irreducibly complex", might eventually have at least a plausible gradual evolutionary path suggested for it. I do sometimes wonder about the required timescales though.

As we have seen, the appearance of design may sometimes be an illusion, and so we need to maintain the distinction between, on the one hand, arguments that there is evidence of intelligent design in the universe (with a small i and a small d) and, on the other hand, the Intelligent Design movement which likes to make much more of the design argument, sometimes when it doesn't seem to me to be justified.

Dawkins' book *The Blind Watchmaker*[69] takes its title from Paley's analogy. Dawkins' proposal is that there is no design, as such, in the world, and that Neo-Darwinism can explain pretty much everything. He gives his own explanation for the evolution of the eye, and for some other items which people formerly said could not have evolved. His overall view is that there is no Paley's "watchmaker" behind the design of the universe, but that "blind" evolution has caused the appearances of design that we observe.

In my view if, in the case of some particular item, there has been insufficient time for the proposed sequence of evolutionary steps to occur, then God may well have designed it. Alternatively if, over a long time period, gradual evolutionary steps genuinely have produced the item in question, then evolution was God's chosen mechanism by which such a thing could happen. Either works for me, because the result is independent of the scientific details. The result is achieved either way, and I wish the biologists well as they try to figure out which way it was from the scientific viewpoint.

The same kinds of arguments about design apply wherever you look. If you look closely at the intricate 'design' of flowers, you can ask whether they were designed like that deliberately, or whether they gradually evolved to be like that as a result of being more successful at getting pollinated. Once again, I would say that God was ultimately responsible either way.

As a final example, I enjoy hill walking, and I especially like being on high, sharp ridges where there are good views straight down into the valleys on both sides. If it's so exposed that it's possible to fall into the valleys, so much the better! Many times, such views will take my breath away and cause me to think of the Creator of it all. In this case, there is probably no controversy about how the views were created. It will have been a combination of lifting and lowering of the land due to movements of Earth's tectonic plates, or volcanic activity arising from a similar source, followed by gradual erosion by wind and water, or more rapid erosion by the effects of glaciation.

However, like looking at the night sky, the fact that the view causes feelings of awe and wonder in me is another indication that God's provision has resulted in a world well suited to our existence. Natural theology has a point, in that such aspects of the natural world, even though we understand them scientifically, really do point us towards God.

Even though we have seen how an illusion of design might arise, that does not do away with the need for God. There is still a valid argument that an intelligent Mind lies behind the 'laws of nature' that we discover by doing science.

We saw earlier that it is rational at least to consider that such an intelligent Designer of the universe may exist and that, if there is such a Designer, he must have existed 'before' he created the universe. Since most scientists believe that both space and time began in the big bang, the word 'before' does not apply in the usual sense. The intelligent Designer must therefore exist separately from space and time as we understand them, and is therefore unlikely to be discovered by the methods of science.

In a similar way, if God has purposes for you and for me, then they are equally unlikely to be susceptible to discovery, or testing, by science; this time, because science can't investigate purposes in the Mind of God.

The next chapter briefly compares the creation story of the last few chapters with the Genesis account in the bible. Also, previous chapters have mentioned several examples of how God might reveal himself though his creation. It would be remiss not to say at least a little about how he might more directly reveal himself to us, so the next chapter says a little more about revelation too.

# Chapter 7  Science, the Bible and Morals

Apart from the scientific story of creation and evolution, the Judeo-Christian creation story in the Bible is the only other one on which I am in any way qualified to pass comment. The interpretation below does have parallels in religions other than Christianity and Judaism though. Also, the last section in this Chapter is completely general, rather than specifically Christian.

As we have noted, a literal reading of the first two chapters of the book of Genesis suggests that God created absolutely everything in six days; efforts by some people to piece together timescales from biblical genealogies date this act of creation at only a few thousand years ago.

The last few chapters have also given an inkling of how comprehensively science has looked into the creation of the universe, including the chemical elements that make it up, and the evolution of life on Earth. The relevant theories are very widely accepted amongst scientists, once they have been carefully and repeatedly tested against observations. Some of those theories have made predictions about discoveries which should be made in the future if they are correct, and the discoveries have duly been made, as predicted.

From earlier chapters it is probably clear that I am happy to accept the scientists' description of the origin of the universe, the galaxies, the stars, The Sun and Earth, including how the chemical elements, of which all those things are made, came into existence. So, how do I reconcile that with the Bible, the handbook of my Christian faith, which may seem to suggest otherwise?

There are various ways of doing it, five of which are briefly reviewed in the Appendix to David Wilkinson's book, *The Message of Creation*.[10] He gives arguments for and against each of the approaches he decided to discuss.

Before looking into this area, it is worth pointing out that if someone wishes to believe that everything we see really was created in six days, a few thousand years ago, then it is certainly not worth falling out over. A genuine relationship with God is more important than discussions about matters such as this. In any case, it is logically acceptable to believe that the days of the book of Genesis were literal 24-hour periods, and there is more than one way of doing so. Here is a way that is logically sound, though I shall explain why I choose not to accept it myself.

Imagine that it is the end of the sixth day of creation, as described in Genesis. Adam and Eve, the first humans, are happily wandering around the Garden of Eden, and God is about to put his feet up for a day of rest.[72] Imagine that you have been transported there in a time machine, and are free to look around and investigate things in a scientific sort of way.

Bearing in mind that Adam and Eve were only created today, how old do they seem to be when you look at them? They are certainly a lot more than a few hours old, since Adam has already been receiving and acting upon instructions from God (Genesis 2:19-20). That was before Eve was even created (Genesis 2:21-22), but we would probably expect Adam and Eve to be of roughly the same age. What can we conclude from this? If Earth really is only six days old, then God must have deliberately created both Adam and Eve as they would be at, say, 20 years of age for the sake of argument. As a whimsical aside, I wonder what memories and ideas would have been in Adam and Eves' '20 year old' minds. If someone wants to buy that idea for a novel from me, just ask!

If you cut down a tree in the Garden of Eden, what would you find inside it? Growth rings, probably, because it is a tree and that's how trees are. The Garden of Eden would not have been much of a garden if it only contained vegetation three days old (vegetation was created on the third day, according to Genesis 1:11-13). So how many rings would you find inside the tree? Let's say 10 – in which case God must have created the tree, three days ago, already looking as if it was 10 years old.

If you were to break open a likely looking rock, you might find a fossil inside. If you happened to have a radioisotope dating kit with you, what kind of age do you think it would suggest for the fossil? Perhaps 200 million years old? Clearly it isn't, since Earth has only existed for six days; God must have created the rock already containing appropriate relative proportions of the products of radioactive decay, such that it has the appearance of being 200 million years old.

You've got the idea by now, but here's just one more thought, which fits in with our previous discussions: say you could get planning permission for a world-class telescope facility in the Garden of Eden. If you pointed such a telescope at the night sky, what would you see? Stars, certainly, because Genesis 1:16 contains the ultimate throw-away sentence, "He also made the stars."

Those stars are only a few days old, but they are many light years away from you, and will therefore appear as such. God must have created them with the beams of photons (starlight) already in place, travelling between the stars and Earth at the speed of light.

You would also see galaxies, and you would find that their light would be suitably red-shifted so that, if you measured their distances and speeds, you would find that they were all moving away from you at speeds proportional to their distances. You would have discovered Hubble's law (Chapter Four). You would conclude that the universe looked about 13.7 billion years old.

So, Earth is really only six days old, but God created it looking much, much older. He would have been consistent in creating everything, and science would later discover the rules that he had put in place.

So far, so good, but there is a theological problem with this kind of idea. Namely, if God is kind and loving, and desires full and meaningful lives for the people whom he has created, why would he deliberately deceive us in this way? It would be the ultimate practical joke, and confirm that he has a sense of humor, but what about the poor scientists? They devote their lives to unpicking the work God has done in creation, in order to understand how Earth and the rest of the universe work, but it all turns out to be a practical joke. I don't think so.

It does point out in the Bible that "the wisdom of this world is foolishness in God's sight",[73] but many scientists are also active, Bible-believing Christians. Surely they cannot all be dismissed as having been side tracked by "the wisdom of this world", by faithfully following the clues God placed in nature.

Many scientists in the past have made statements similar to that of Johannes Kepler, who said, when he was doing his science, that he was, "Thinking God's thoughts after him." Indeed, the modern scientific method arose from the work of such scientists, who were firm believers in God as the Creator of the universe, and decided to devote their lives to understanding as much as they could of how he had gone about making it work. The same impulse drives many scientists today. So, would you be interested in worshiping the sort of god who would deliberately deceive us all?

The results of careful scientific investigation would be expected to be verifiable and consistent, if a consistently reliable God had created the universe. For many people, including me, the fact that the behavior of the universe is sufficiently regular for us to be able to discover the underlying laws of nature, and sufficiently consistent for us to be able simply to assume that they apply everywhere, as we do, is a very good indicator that it was created, and is maintained in being, by a faithful, supreme Creator.

I cannot seriously believe that such a Creator would then be so capricious as to trick all the astrophysicists, cosmologists, evolutionary biologists, geologists, paleontologists and others, into spending their lives on a wild goose chase, the results of which are a complete illusion.

So, I am sticking to the belief that the well-verified findings of science are genuine, and I therefore need to find a different way of interpreting those first two chapters of the Bible. If someone is happy to stick with a literal interpretation, despite all the evidence to the contrary, and the fact that it means that God has deliberately tricked us, then nobody can logically disprove that view. They can only protest on theological grounds, such as those put forward above.

The first way out of this problem that I came across, in my late teenage years, hinges upon the fact that the word translated as "day" in Genesis, can apparently mean any period of time.[74] If the "days" of Genesis each cover millions, or even billions, of years then, as we shall see shortly, Genesis might actually agree surprisingly well with the scientific description of creation, given how old the Genesis sources are.

That kind of idea kept me happy for several years, although I have recognized some difficulties with it since then. One potential problem is that, as Wilkinson points out, the use of "day" in this passage really does seem to be tied in with mornings and evenings, and as part of a week.

On the other hand, Victor Pierce, in his book *Evidence for Truth: Science,* [75] suggests that the Hebrew word *diger*, translated as "morning", literally means "beginning", whilst *aered*, translated as "evening", means "conclusion". If Pierce is correct in this, it isn't necessary to understand "morning" and "evening" as marking off

24-hour days in a week, since Pearce's alternative translations would simply mark off the beginnings and ends of variable periods of time. However, I am not qualified to discuss the detailed interpretation of ancient texts, so I'll leave that to the experts.

## How do science and Genesis compare?

The material that follows is based on a table in Pierce's book,[75] and the text accompanying it. The information is interesting, but I think that this kind of approach is misguided overall, which is why it is only stated very briefly – you'll need to read Pierce's book for the full version.

As in Pierce's presentation, there follows a list of some brief quotations from Genesis (New International Version) in the sequence in which they appear in the Bible, compared with the findings of science.

The sources for the book of Genesis are very old. Wilkinson suggests that those for the first chapter of Genesis were written about 500 to 600 years BC, whilst those for the story in the second chapter of Genesis date from about 900 to 1000 years BC. To put this into context, it places the writing of Genesis 1 in the early Iron Age, and the earlier Genesis 2 in the Bronze Age.

Given this fact, as Pierce points out, it is remarkable that whilst other cultures' creation stories are based upon wild guesses, Genesis has a sequence of events which agrees fairly well with modern science. He suggests that this is evidence that the writers of Genesis were inspired by the Creator of the universe, otherwise they would have been very unlikely to get it so correct, writing so long before the emergence of modern science.

Genesis 1:1 says, "In the beginning God created the heavens and the Earth." Science says that the big bang did it but, if we believe that the Mind behind the big bang was God, then both are correct.

Genesis 1:2 says, "The earth was formless and empty, darkness was over the surface of the deep." Science suggests that Earth and The Sun condensed out of clouds of hot gas and that Earth probably passed through a liquid state. For a long time Earth would have been surrounded by a thick atmosphere, keeping out whatever light there may be.

Genesis 1:3 says, "God said, 'Let there be light', and there was light." Science says that as Earth and The Sun condensed, The Sun (being sufficiently massive) reached a stage at which the temperature at its center was high enough to start nuclear fusion reactions – it became a star and began to shine.

Genesis 1:6-8 says, "God said, 'Let there be an expanse between the waters ...' and separated the water under the expanse from the water above it. ... God called the expanse 'sky'." When Earth first became cool enough, water vapor from the atmosphere (the "sky") would have condensed as rain, producing rivers and seas on the surface.

Genesis 1:9-10 says, "God said, 'Let the water under the sky be gathered to one place, and let dry ground appear.' ... God called the dry ground 'land', and the gathered waters he called 'seas'." There was originally a single landmass on Earth - the supercontinent Pangaea. Only later did continental drift (plate tectonics) create the continents as we see them now.

Genesis 1:11 says, "God said, 'Let the land produce vegetation ... '." At first sight, this seems to be out of sequence, but Pierce suggests that "Earth" (as used in the Authorized Version of the Bible) is a better translation than "land", and that the Hebrew word *deshe* should not be translated as "vegetation" since it simply means "greenness". With those modifications, Pierce suggests that Genesis 1:11 is about green algae in the sea, creating the oxygen for Earth's atmosphere. If he is correct, then this is also in agreement with the scientific sequence of events.

Genesis 1:11 also says, "God said, 'Let the land produce vegetation: seed-bearing plants and trees on the land that bear fruit with seed in it ...'." Again, this seems out of sequence, as the fossil record tells us that marine life appeared before land-based vegetation. Pierce has an explanation based on the grouping together of the biological order of plant life, but I didn't find that one particularly convincing.

Genesis 1:16 says, "God made two great lights – the greater light to govern the day and the lesser light to govern the night. He also made the stars." Pierce states that the Hebrew here contains an "historic tense" meaning that The Sun, Moon and stars were already in existence. The passage is then said to be written from the viewpoint of a hypothetical person on Earth's surface. As the thick, misty atmosphere cleared, The Sun, Moon and stars would have become visible, in that order, rather than just their diffused light.

Genesis 1:20 says, "God said, 'Let the water teem with living creatures, and let birds fly above the Earth ...'." Many think that life began in the seas, so that's OK. Pearce suggests that the word that is translated "birds" would be better translated as "flying creatures", which is probably intended as "insects". If so, that's about right, too.

Incidentally, here Pierce raises what he sees to be a problem for evolution, in that insects and flowers need each other to survive, so how could they have evolved separately? The evolutionists have a simple answer to that one though: wind pollination was probably the first way of doing it but, after insects arrived, their pollination was much more efficient than relying on the wind so, after that, natural selection favored flowers and insects with close relationships.

Genesis 1:21-23 says, "God created the great creatures of the sea and every living and moving thing with which the water teems ... and every winged bird ...". Note that "the great creatures of the sea" could include such creatures as the plesiosaurus.

Genesis 1:24-25 says, "Let the land produce living creatures ... : livestock, creatures that move along the ground and wild animals ... ."

Genesis 1:26-27 says, "God said, 'Let us make man in our image ...' ... male and female he created them."

I am not able to pass any scholarly comment on Pierce's various suggestions, but these comparisons do indicate that, perhaps with just one or two exceptions, everything else can be argued to tie in fairly well with the description according to twenty-first century science. Contrary to the tendency of many atheists to simply dismiss Genesis, this is actually fairly impressive for such early documents, written when other cultures believed that Earth was supported by giant turtles, elephants or snakes for example; or believed that Earth was formed as the result of a battle between warring gods; or worshiped The Sun, Moon, stars, or features of Earth, as gods.

## Is that the best approach?

After thinking from time to time, over a period of several years, about the types of discussion mentioned in the previous section, I eventually decided that the best approach is to avoid trying to justify the exact words written in Genesis – otherwise I begin to fall into my self-defined trap of trying to interpret Genesis as a scientific text book which, given its age, it cannot have been intended to be.

Instead, as suggested in Chapter One, perhaps it is best to regard Genesis as poetic literature with a purpose, rather than as a literal, step-by-step, historical or scientific narrative. At the time Genesis was written, few people could read or write. The way in which they remembered important information from their history was similar to the way in which many people who enter memory competitions memorize things today. They weave the important information into a story, often a journey. The start of the story reminds them of the first thing, then the next part the second, and so on.

That is, broadly speaking, the way in which many scholars believe Genesis to have been written. It is a story written to record important information about God and his relationship with Earth and with us, in a memorable form. We saw, in Chapter One, that the Bible is a library of different kinds of literature, but that we should not expect to find a science text in it. Genesis was never intended to be a literal, step-by-step, scientific record of events.

If Genesis had been pitched at the level of understanding of a later age, such as ours, it would simply have been nonsense to its early users. There would have been no point in writing it like that at that time.

Another thing that I soon realized is that, although the relationship between modern science and religion is of interest to me, it is a matter of some boredom to many others. It seems that many people don't really need a scientific description of the world so all this is less problematic for them than it was for me.

Such people are just not particularly interested in science and technology, perhaps directing their interest instead to the arts and humanities. Some are happy to take on trust whatever the 'wisdom of the age' is, as handed down by the scientists. They simply enjoy the labor saving, health-care, transportation, computing, energy and utilities, communications and entertainment technologies, without any need to appreciate how they work, or from where they came.

More seriously, quite apart from lacking the inclination, some people simply don't have the intellectual capacity for the high-level study of science. As a Christian, I firmly believe that Jesus is relevant to everyone, at whatever level is appropriate to their circumstances. In many cases that will rule out the need for any intellectual justification of how science and religion can co-exist.

For those who don't require such justification, much of the material in books like this one is no more than a sideshow. Even for those who do like some justification, it remains much less important than their relationship with God. It only assumes greater significance if they genuinely need some technical answers to help them on their way to that relationship.

Therefore, although many people are keen to understand as much as they can about how the world works and, if they are religious, what their god has to do with that, such an outlook is not a prerequisite for everyone. As I know very well from conversations with some of my friends, including my wife, I am in a minority.

All of that being the case, we should not really expect any part of a holy book in general, or the Bible in particular, to require interpretation as a science text. Instead, it does make sense to view Genesis as more of a poetical description of creation and, in particular, to follow Wilkinson's assessment of Genesis, as quoted in Chapter One.

Wilkinson has other interesting things to say about Genesis too. For example, he discusses Genesis 1:16, which we looked at above, "God made two great lights – the greater light to govern the day and the lesser light to govern the night. He also made the stars." Wilkinson asks, why did the writer, inspired by God, not simply name The Sun and The Moon, and why the throwaway line about the stars?[76] His suggestion is that many of the surrounding nations would have worshiped some, or all, of The Sun, Moon and stars as gods. By deliberately not even gracing The Sun and Moon with names, and by dismissing the stars so briefly, the writer was making it clear that God is the only god, and the creator of everything, including the things that those other nations regarded as gods.

The Genesis account and the scientific account of creation are complementary to each other. The scientific account tells us how it happened, and the Genesis account introduces us to the Creator who decided that it should happen. The fact that there is actually a fair amount of 'technical' agreement between Genesis and the scientific account is a bonus, which strengthens the view that the first part of Genesis was inspired by the same Mind whose ideas of creation are still being discovered by science today.

The last few chapters have demonstrated that science has a good handle on what happened in the big bang, and also on the developments since then, but that it does not attempt to tell us why. On the other hand, from a Christian viewpoint, the Bible tells us why it happened, in the sense that God decided to do it, in order that creatures (we, as it happens) would come to exist who could have a loving relationship with him. Genesis also begins to tell us more about God as the supreme Mind behind everything that is.

Perhaps you still take the view that everything described in the scientific sections of these chapters 'just happened' by chance, but I hope that you can also see why, even today, it is still rational to argue that God could be the originator of the universe. The 'god of the gaps' argument still applies to specific details, but not to the overall suggestion that creation was God's idea.

I favor the viewpoint that there is a supreme Creator who desired that such a remarkable universe should come into existence, and such a viewpoint is beyond the possibility of disproof by science. Some of the evidence from these chapters, and the rest of the book, is summed up in the closing chapter. The awe and wonder that many of us experience when trying to think about the complexity and scale of the universe is a good reason for worshiping such a Creator. There is more to come in the following chapters too.

## What does Christ have to do with creation?

What do Christians believe about the role of Jesus Christ in creation? Readers of other faiths may disagree with some of the sentiments in this section, but at least the logic should be clear. There is also an introduction to the Christian view of suffering. The next section returns to more general material.

If God exists and wants to have a relationship with us, it would be extremely surprising if he had left us completely without any pointers to his existence, or hints as to how that relationship might come about.

The approach of natural theology is to look at the natural world and to try to infer from it the existence of God. Insofar as it gives us clues to his existence, that's fine, several have already been mentioned and there are more to come later. However, it can never go the whole way, because of the general difficulty of proof, which we have come across several times.

So God has always revealed himself in his creation, but more is needed. In pre-Christian times, for example, the Jewish faith claims that God revealed himself through the various prophets, and others, and dealt with the people in that way.

Christianity claims that, in Jesus, something very different happened. Here is an abridged version of the opening verses of John's gospel from the new testament of the Bible:[77]

> In the beginning was the Word, and the Word was with God, and the Word was God. He was with God in the beginning.
>
> Through him all things were made; without him nothing was made that has been made. In him was life, and that life was the light of men. The light shines in the darkness, but the darkness has not understood it.

> There came a man who was sent from God; his name was John.[78]
> He came as a witness to testify concerning that light, so that through him all men might believe. ... The true light that gives light to every man was coming into the world.
>
> He was in the world, and ... the world was made through him ...
>
> ... The Word became flesh and made his dwelling among us. We have seen his glory, the glory of the One and Only, who came from the Father, full of grace and truth.

This is not going to be a bible study on this passage;[79] the next few paragraphs simply point out the features most relevant to our discussion.

The expression "the Word" which first appears right at the beginning (in more senses than one) is a translation of the word *logos* that was used in Greek philosophy to represent the rationality underlying the universe.

Following the logic through the quotation above, the first two paragraphs contain a transition from "Word", through "life" to "light", and the third paragraph points out that John the Baptist testified as to the coming of that "light" into the world – later culminating in his baptism of Jesus, who later referred to himself as "the light of the world".[80] Together with the final paragraph above, it is clear that John (the gospel writer) is equating Jesus with "the Word".

That being the case, the passage above tells us that Jesus was there "with God" at the beginning of everything,[81] and that nothing that was created was created without him.

The bible therefore teaches (as summarized in the quoted passage) that Jesus, whilst he was on Earth, was God in human form ("made flesh"). In terms of creation, Jesus, as worshiped by Christians, therefore reveals to us what the Creator is like, and how we should live as part of his creation.

The comparison between what Jesus reveals to us about God, and what we might discover about God from other sources, such as studying his creation in a scientific way, is neatly summarized by the following illustration from Wilkinson's *The Message of Creation*.[10]

"An evangelist tells the story of when he was a child seeing his parents about to destroy an ant-nest with a pan of boiling water. He ran down the garden to the nest and tried to warn the ants. He shouted, explained what was going to happen and motioned with his arms. It was, of course, no good and the ants did not see their warm bath coming and take avoiding action. He came to the conclusion that the only way he could have saved the ants was if he had become an ant."

The obvious parallel is that God, in the person of Jesus, became a human in order to be able to communicate with us in a new way, which we could easily understand. He could then directly tell us, both by what he said and by what he did, much more than we would ever learn from prophets, or by studying the world around us, and the universe at large.

Jesus is, as certainly as anything else in history, an historical character, as confirmed by non-Christian historians of the period, such as Josephus (Jewish) and Tacitus (Roman). In terms of Christian documents, the earliest manuscripts for the New Testament gospels, and Paul's letters, are deemed to be much more reliable than any other documents of similar age, for a number of reasons.

Firstly, they were all written down when the number of surviving eye witnesses to Jesus' ministry began to seriously decline, namely within about 70 years of Jesus' death. Some were probably written at least twenty years earlier than that.[82]

Secondly, when the gospels were written, especially the earliest ones, there would still have been several people alive who had witnessed Jesus' teaching, and would have challenged the gospel accounts if they were false.

Thirdly, there are many more different early copies of the manuscripts, than is the case for any other ancient writing. These have been cross-referenced to remove a few minor copying errors.

Fourthly, the population at that time was skilled at passing on information orally, so there had not yet been sufficient time for embellishments and legends to build up.

According to those gospels (and other books of the New Testament), Jesus said, and did, plenty of things intended to confirm that he is one with God.

Discussions about this usually result in three possibilities. Either Jesus was mentally ill, as we tend to regard people to be today if they claim to be God; or he was evil in that he was simply lying and performing illusions; or he was telling the truth. I am satisfied that he was telling the truth, and therefore that Jesus Christ reveals to us what God is like, and what he requires of us.

In the next chapter we shall be looking at more of the things which the scientists have discovered about the universe, and which might also suggest that God had something to do with the origin of it.

To end this section, here is a little about the problem of suffering in God's creation. Christians believe that God understands and shares in their suffering. Later, we shall see that he understands it at a far higher level than we can hope to do.

However, the Bible tells us, and the experience of Christians confirms it, that God also comes alongside us in our suffering, and understands our problems. This is most obvious in the life of Jesus, who was born in squalor, shared the usual sufferings of a human life, including hunger, thirst, doubt, rejection, and hitting his thumb with a hammer in the carpenter's shop (I don't have a Bible reference for the last of those, unfortunately).

He also went out of his way to remove the suffering of others wherever he could and, most of all, took on an unusual amount of suffering himself at the end of his earthly life, culminating in torture and his painful death nailed to a cross.

Not only does God understand, and participate in suffering, but he can also turn it into good. For Christians, perhaps the ultimate example is that the death of Jesus led to his resurrection and the hope of new life for us in him. Some of the evidence that the resurrection actually took place is mentioned briefly in Chapter 11.

Many of us have also experienced bad being turned to good, in our own small ways. I suffered a serious motorcycle accident in 1982, which resulted in some spells in hospital, a number of operations on my right leg, spread over a period of about 18 months, a lot of serious pain, a few months off work, and some residual problems which continue to the present. However, at least three good things came out of that experience.

Least importantly, I managed to write up most of my PhD thesis during the period when I was off work, including whilst I was in hospital with my leg in traction – much to the amusement of the nurses, who couldn't understand where all that incomprehensible technical stuff was coming from! Since I was doing a responsible full-time job in industry at the same time as my PhD, and had a young family, I'm not sure when else I could have written-up the thesis.

The next thing that I remember is that several of the other patients in that orthopedic ward were much worse off than I. That very concrete confirmation that there are always people much worse off than I has never left me.

Most importantly, you might think that I would have questioned God during such an experience, with the "why me?" sort of questions (especially as the accident was not my fault). You might also think that my faith would have suffered as a result. In fact, such a question never entered my head, and my Christian faith was, strangely, significantly strengthened during that experience. I believe that God was responding to a lot of my friends who were praying for me.

God knows about our suffering and pain, and comes alongside us in them. He can also bring good things out of the bad, and strengthen our faith through them. We also have the hope that, through Christ, we shall always ultimately overcome them. Suffering and pain will not have the last word.

Now we return to the less explicitly Christian material.

## The moral law

Whilst working full-time in the University, I had a physicist colleague who told me that the types of consideration mentioned in this section were more important than any technical arguments, in his renouncing atheism and deciding to become a Christian.

The phrase, "the moral law", is borrowed from the sermons of John Wesley and the writings of C.S. Lewis, particularly Lewis' classic book, *Mere Christianity*.[83] Some of what follows is loosely based on Lewis' treatment of the subject. [84]

If you listen to a couple of children playing with toys, it is usually not very long before one of them will say, "That's not fair." In small children, you might just put that down to selfishness but, except in really young children, it's not that simple.

For example, if one child is complaining because the other has a toy which she wants, it is quite likely that the complaining child knows that the other child also has a right to play with the toy. She is complaining not simply because he has it and she does not, but because he has monopolized it for too long and so it is reasonable that she should now be allowed to play with it for some time instead.

It is also possible that, if this were explained to the other child, he would agree that he had had more than his fair share of the toy. Nevertheless, he may still refuse to give it up.

The same patterns of behavior apply when we are adults. Imagine that you have been waiting in a queue for a long time. If someone arrives and 'pushes in' to the queue ahead of you, your immediate reaction is likely to be, "That's not fair." Why should someone else be allowed to shortcut the procedure that you, and everyone else in the queue, have had to go through? If pushers-in are challenged about this behavior, it usually becomes clear that they also know that their behavior is unacceptable.

A more interesting kind of example occurs when, for instance, you are shopping and you notice that there is only one item remaining, of something that you need. You hurry towards it, but someone gets there before you and picks it up.

You will probably feel annoyed about the fact that you have missed that item, but you won't think of blaming the other person, and you won't say that it is unfair, because you know that the other person had just as much right as you to pick up the item.

Now imagine, instead, that you got to that last item ahead of anyone else, picked it up and put it in your supermarket trolley. Then, when you turned round to pick up another item, someone who had seen you pick up the last item, removed it from your trolley and put it into their own. You would now definitely say that this was unfair.

If you complained to that person, they would not normally stand their ground and argue the case that you had not paid for the item, that it therefore wasn't yet yours, and that they were therefore as entitled to take it from your trolley as from the shelf. They would know that what they had done was unacceptable.

These are very trivial examples, and you might be thinking that this kind of thing is simply social convention, and has no deeper meaning than that. However, that might not be the case. John Polkinghorne has a very good point when he says, in his book *Science and Christian Belief*, [85] "Although atheism might seem simpler ... conceptually, it treats beauty and morals and worship as some form of cultural or social brute facts, which accords ill with the seriousness with which these experiences touch us as persons." The moral law (and beauty and worship) affect our lives at a much deeper level than can adequately be explained simply by cultural or social convention.

C.S. Lewis also got it right when he suggested that, although we might learn some aspects of the moral law, "From parents and teachers, and friends and books, as we learn everything else", the moral law belongs to a particular type of knowledge. He pointed out that some of the things we learn in that way, such as driving on the left-hand side of the road (in Britain), are, "Mere conventions which might have been different", for example if we live in a country where people drive on the right-hand side of the road.

On the other hand, things such as multiplication tables or mathematics are, "Real truths" which just exist out there, in an absolute form for everyone, whether we learn them or not. The moral law belongs to the latter category.

Britain may well, in general, be a world center-of-excellence for orderly queuing; there are some countries in which people are much more likely to push into queues, ahead of people already queuing, than they are in Britain. However, even in those countries, the local people still resent being pushed back in the queue by latecomers. Although there may be a local convention that queues, in those cultures, are less sacrosanct than they are in Britain, there is also some higher-level law at work, which still makes people realize that there is some injustice going on.

Taking a broader view, you might say that orderly and cooperative behavior keeps society well ordered and smooth running, so it is to the benefit of society, and we must do it to avoid chaos. However, the question then becomes, why should any individual care about what is good for society, if it does not benefit her directly? For example, I could say, "Why shouldn't I fight for the last item on the supermarket shelf, or the last space on the bus? In that moment, it makes no difference at all to me whether or not it affects 'society'." You might well reply, "Because you ought to consider others, and act in a less selfish way." That's the moral law at work in you.

In addressing the point that different cultures, and different times, have had different moralities, Lewis said (in the 1940s – but the argument is still valid), "There have been differences between their moralities, but these have never amounted to anything like a total difference. If anyone will take the trouble to compare the moral teaching of, say, the ancient Egyptians, Babylonians, Hindus, Chinese, Greeks and Romans, what will really strike him will be how very like they are to each other and to our own."

He goes on to say, "Think [about] what a totally different morality would mean. Think of a country where people were admired for running away in battle, or where a man felt proud of double-crossing all the people who had been kindest to him ... Men have differed as regards what people you ought to be unselfish to – whether it was only your own family, or your fellow countrymen, or every one. But they have always agreed that you ought not to put yourself first. Selfishness has never been admired. Men have differed as to whether you should have one wife or four. But they have always agreed that you must not simply have any woman you liked."

People are also prone to operate double standards. Someone who says that there is no absolute right or wrong will, nevertheless, have some internal absolute standard against which he judges things. For example, he may happily break a promise that he made to you but, if you break one that you made to him, he will complain about it. If he really has no absolute standard, and is happy that promises can be broken, then against what standard is he making the judgment that you ought to keep your promise to him?

Similarly, although different cultures may disagree over the detail of what they consider to be right or wrong, most reasonable people, from any culture, would agree that there are some things that are always wrong. As a fairly extreme example, the vast majority of people, the world over, would agree that torturing children for fun would always be wrong.

Some people might attempt to make excuses to themselves about why it is acceptable for them to do such things but, if they are rational, in their heart of hearts they will know that they are wrong. To demonstrate that they are wrong, it would only be necessary to ask them, if they have the right to do such things to someone else, does someone else have the right to do such things to them? They would say no, thus admitting that such things are too unpleasant to be done to them and therefore, by implication, that they would be wrong to do them to anyone else. They admit that there is a moral standard, even if they selfishly choose not to apply it.

As a final example here, even in a society that culturally allows certain injustices, people do know that they are wrong, but many people can easily suppress that knowledge since the culture allows it. For example, until relatively recently, it was acceptable to use people as slaves in several cultures. However, as long ago as Roman times, there were those who urged their contemporaries at least to treat their slaves well. It was also recognized that, in certain circumstances, slaves could be given their freedom; thus acknowledging some absolute standard (the moral law) which says that freedom is better than slavery, even though the culture, as a whole, was happy to suppress that standard and propagate the practice of slavery.

In more recent times, some brave souls began to speak out against the whole slave-owning and slave-trading status quo. That caused others to become more aware of the promptings of the moral law, in opposition to embedded cultural practices, with the result that slavery was eventually abolished pretty much all over the world. The moral law had always been there, but it had been made easy for people to suppress its promptings because of the culture that prevailed. Quoting Lewis again, "Human beings, all over the Earth, have this curious idea that they ought to behave in a certain way, and cannot really get rid of it."

Interestingly, even though we have a good idea of this moral law of what is right or wrong, we don't always obey it. For example, although we know that nobody is admired for being selfish, that is exactly what many of us are a lot of the time. Perhaps most of us don't do it to excess, but it is very easy to put ourselves before others more than we should.

Some will say that this kind of thing is simply because we evolved from lower animals, where the law of, "Nature, red in tooth and claw"[86] applies. In nature, it is often necessary to compete for food to survive, and it is also often the strongest and most aggressive male who wins the right to mate with the most females, and thus passes on his genes to the next generation.

Because his genes contain some successful coding for being aggressive and winning mates, that coding propagates into future generations and, presumably, such genes were present in the first humans and persist to the present day, in us, in some form. If there were to be some major catastrophe in a westernized society, resulting in the total loss of mains electricity (and hence gas, water and fuel too because of the inability to run compressors and pumps), many people would suppress the moral law and revert to type in the face of death from cold, thirst and starvation.

However, despite that, humans appear to live on a completely different plane of consciousness from any other creature. There is probably no other creature on Earth which is capable of contemplating its own existence, of knowing that it is doing so, of thinking about where it came from, or what purpose it might have in life; thinking about how it ought to behave, or the fact that it will die some day; and wondering what might happen after that.

Perhaps there is no other species whose males are capable of reasoning that being kind and generous, rather than over-assertive, aggressive and violent, might be an equally good strategy for forming relationships. That kind of behavior does seem to happen, to some extent, in other species, but perhaps it only comes about by chance there, rather than as the result of any rational thought process. We, on the other hand, are definitely capable of thinking it out, and choosing how to behave as a result.

We humans seem to have the ability to overcome some of the primitive programming that persists in our genes, and I suggest that God has provided the means by which we do so. Yes, we may sometimes feel aggressive towards somebody, but the moral law whispers to us that we should not take any violent action; we can choose to walk away. Yes, we can feel attracted towards someone else's girlfriend, boyfriend, husband, or wife, but the moral law lets us know that we shouldn't go there. Even in the doomsday scenario described three paragraphs ago, there would be those who continued to heed the moral law, even though they would suffer for it.

The point of all this is to illustrate that we are aware of a moral law which lets us know which things are wrong, but often we choose to disobey it, and to do the wrong things anyway. It is quite likely that you have not committed any major damage or crime as a result. But we can all think of times when we could have behaved in a better way, and not necessarily years ago either, perhaps just yesterday. There is a story of a Christian who prayed one day, along the lines of, "Dear God, I thank you that I haven't said anything wrong today, I haven't done anything wrong today, I haven't even thought anything wrong today. All I have thought about is you ... However, I am about to get out of bed, and all that will change!"

If you know you have not behaved in the best way possible, that is an indication that a standard exists; if you know that you could have behaved better, then you acknowledge a standard by which you judge some behavior to be better than some other behavior. Some aspects of that standard may, indeed, be set by local culture, but there are universally accepted aspects to it too.

Lewis also points out that there is another thing about the moral law, which distinguishes it from the other instincts and feelings that we might have. It often prompts us to choose between two competing instincts, and often prompts us to follow the weaker of the two. In other words, it modifies our behavior in ways that might not be to our own advantage.

He puts it like this, "Feeling a desire to help [another person] is quite different from feeling that you ought to help whether you want to or not. Supposing you hear a cry for help from a man in danger. You will probably feel two desires – one a desire to give help (due to your herd instinct),[87] the other a desire to keep out of danger (due to the instinct for self-preservation). But you will find inside you, in addition to these two impulses, a third thing which tells you that you ought to follow the impulse to help, and suppress the impulse to run away."

Lewis also points out that it is necessary to have this absolute, higher-level, arbitrating law because none of our normal instincts is suitable in all circumstances. For example, usually, as a normal member of society, the instinct to fight needs to be suppressed but, if someone attacks your children for example, it may need to come to the fore.

Even an instinct that is generally wholly good, such as keeping your children from harm, sometimes needs tempering with different behavior. Although you might want your children never to come to any harm, you also know that it is better for them to be exposed to some every-day level of danger, rather than being locked away from it in a padded cell, otherwise they will never learn how to look after themselves.

In summary, the moral law is a truth that exists independently of anything we humans may have invented. It is difficult to tie it down into a list of specific 'dos and don'ts', indeed that would defeat the whole argument as the moral law gives us an over-arching knowledge of what is right and wrong, independently of any cultural rules and regulations, and sometimes (as in the example of the slave-trade) even in opposition to cultural conventions. It also prompts us to 'do the right thing', when to do so may be to our disadvantage, and may even put us in danger. I believe that this law comes from God.

We have also seen that, although we are aware of this law of how we *ought* to behave, we sometimes choose not behave in accordance with it. God understands that we will struggle always to keep that law in our own strength, so he is willing to enter our lives, fill that God-shaped hole inside us, and enable us to do so, if we invite him in.

# Chapter 8  What is the Fine-Tuning of the Universe?

This chapter looks at the phenomenon of fine-tuning of the universe, whilst the next provides a few examples of the many unlikely coincidences which needed to happen in order for there to be a universe, and for that universe to be capable of supporting a planet with life. The question implicit in these chapters is whether these really are just coincidences, or whether it might be easier to believe that God had something to do with them.

## What does "fine-tuning" mean?

A good example of a system that requires tuning is a pre-digital radio receiver. You need to turn the dial to just the right place on the frequency scale in order to be able receive the station you want to hear. That is very easy, because there is only one dial to adjust, and the sensitivity with which it needs to be set is within your capability to achieve.

By way of a more demanding example, when working as a control systems engineer I have often had to tune a controller to get the best possible response out of some system or other. For example, imagine a motor that needs to be controlled in order to drive the arm of a robot to a particular position.

It is usually best if the robot's arm reaches the required position as quickly as possible, and then stops quickly and accurately without overshooting the required position. Unfortunately, such requirements usually conflict with each other – for example, the faster the robot is allowed to move, the harder it is to stop it at the required position without any overshoot. If it did overshoot, it would then have to reverse to get back to the correct position, and may oscillate for a while before coming to rest.

In addition, the controller will usually have several parameters which need to be tuned simultaneously in order to try to obtain the required performance, and it may not be clear how best to do that, because the various settings will interact. A tolerable performance achieved by setting two dials may be spoiled by adjusting a third; yet, with the third in a different position, an even better performance might then be achieved by re-tuning the first two – or it might not.

In any industrial control system with many variable parameters to be set simultaneously, it is going to be difficult to get the best result; sometimes, it is even difficult to define what the best result would be. This is clearly a much more difficult proposition than tuning a radio, to the extent that many industrial control systems remain less well-tuned than they could be; but it is a completely trivial problem compared with trying to tune a universe.

We saw, in Chapter One, that the universe has a number of fundamental constants, which need to have particular numerical values in order for the universe to exist as we know it. Some people have suggested viewing these fundamental constants of nature as adjustable 'dials', which must have been set to specific values in order for the universe to behave as it does. The difficulty is that there are many such dials to be set simultaneously; that is a very thorny problem.

We currently have little idea as to how much interaction there might be between the values of the fundamental constants of nature, taken as a complete set; or whether there is more than just the one set of values which would lead to a universe supporting life as we know it.

So, in the context of this chapter, "tuning" is the adjustment of the imaginary dials that set the values of the fundamental constants of the universe. It is a sensible analogy, because the universe does have these fundamental numbers, and they do have the 'dial settings' that scientists have measured. The question is, were the dials set by a 'cosmic designer', did the complete set of values just appear by chance, or is there some explanation in between those extremes?

"Fine"-tuning, in the context of the universe, refers to the apparent need for some of these fundamental constants to have extremely precise values. In other words, some of the dials needed to be set much more accurately than the dial on your radio, to an extraordinary degree of precision, and they probably all needed to be set simultaneously, otherwise the universe couldn't exist as we know it.

## Are simple explanations enough?

In addition to the comments in the previous section, some of the things we have seen earlier have also indicated that we live in a universe well suited to our existence. This begs the question: why is Earth so finely tuned as to allow our existence?

For example, why is the temperature range just right? Why are the atmospheric conditions just right for the carbon cycle, the water cycle, the weather patterns and everything else that keeps Earth working as we need it to? Why is the atmosphere thick enough to cause most meteors which come our way to burn up before they hit the ground – and give us spectacular 'shooting stars' to look at whilst they do so? Why is Earth's magnetic field such that it deflects most of the harmful particles radiated from The Sun? Why is gravity just right? Why are the values of the other fundamental constants of nature fixed so that the universe has evolved in a manner that is just right for Earth to be just as it is? The list of such questions can become very long indeed.

One catch-all answer to such questions, usually called an "anthropic principle", is that Earth simply has to be the way it is. There is no alternative because, if it were any other way, we would not exist. Turning the argument around, because we are here to ask these questions, the conditions in the universe must be exactly those conditions that suit our survival. No matter how improbable it may seem that more than twenty 'dials' have each been set very carefully indeed, the conditions simply could not be much different from what they are, or we would not be here to discuss it.

This is an interesting observation, and presumably it is true, but it doesn't seem to be particularly helpful. If we are looking for help in understanding the universe, this observation seems to contain no information that we do not already have. In other words, it just says, "things are as they are because they are", but it makes no suggestions which actually help us to understand why that might be the case.

A related argument is that any seemingly special values in the universe, such as the amount of gravitational attraction between any two bodies seeming to be "just right", are actually illusions due to an observer selection effect. That means that we only ask such questions because we, due to our special position as observers of the situation, are biased into thinking that those values are somehow more special than they actually are.

Imagine that you were to find yourself sitting next to a stranger at a concert, got friendly with them, and eventually married them and spent the rest of your life with them. Looking back, you might be convinced that there was something special about the fact that you found yourself sitting next to that person.

Maybe there was, but it is more likely that you both bought your tickets at a similar time, for example – the feeling that something special happened is probably just a selection effect. You had to sit next to someone, and it just happened to be that person. Only the subsequent events, and your relationship with that person make it seem more special than all the other times you've sat next to a stranger.

Those who are aware of the selection effect might point out that the settings of the dials that govern the fate of the universe can be viewed in exactly the same way as the example above. The various physical constants, which make the universe suitable for us to live in it, each had to have some value or other, and they just happen to have the values we observe.

They would say that it is all just a coincidence, but that we tend to think that the values must be special in some way because we exist here, and now, to be able to talk about them, whereas we wouldn't be here to do so it if the values had been different.

The underlying suggestion is that we are a coincidence, along with the numbers. Our existence is nothing special, we just happen to be here because the numbers dropped out from the infinite set of possibilities in the way that they did. From a purely scientific viewpoint, no matter how improbable the situation becomes as more and more 'dials' are added to those which need to be set, the anthropic principle argument, and the suggestion of a selection effect, remain valid.

However, we have seen several times in this book that a purely scientific account of the universe is inadequate as a complete explanation. In the present case, the anthropic argument seems to be a correct statement of fact, but it doesn't seem to tell us anything. The selection effect is undoubtedly a genuine phenomenon in humans, but its applicability to this argument, as with many other suggestions we have come across, cannot be either proved or disproved scientifically.

The more the improbabilities stack up, the more difficult it becomes for many people, including me, to accept the selection effect argument – even though I understand that that is the whole point of the argument! Just because the situation is such that there possibly could be a selection effect operating, doesn't mean that there necessarily is.

The rest of the chapter should demonstrate that it is, indeed, extremely improbable that we should have come to exist. Nevertheless, we have. Most people would agree so far. To me, it seems that the answer to the question "why?" eventually boils down to one of two types of scenario, which is where we may begin to disagree.

The first kind of scenario is based on the notion that "why?" is a silly question to ask. Supporters of this idea might say, for example, that there is nothing special about the fact that we are here, it is just a happy accident – enjoy it. The fact that it seems as though there was something special about the initial conditions at the big bang really is just a selection effect.

They may say that there are probably infinitely many possibilities for the initial conditions of the universe at the big bang, and hence for the number of different universes which might have come into existence. A universe in which we could evolve was obviously one of those possibilities, and it just happens to be the one that occurred. It's like winning a lottery against phenomenally long odds – it is almost impossible that we should have won, the probability being almost zero, but someone had to win and, in this case, it just happened to be us.

The other kind of scenario invokes the idea that there is an intelligent mind behind the universe, who decided to create it, and who set up the initial conditions for the big bang so that the desired kind of universe would result.

I don't think there is a watertight logical argument against either of those possibilities, but there is also the interesting question as to whether everything that has had to happen since the big bang, leading up to the existence of you and me, is equally covered by the two possibilities.

It probably is, but my own inclination is to sharpen-up the second possibility such that the "intelligent mind" is God, and to suggest that he desired to create creatures able to have a loving relationship with him. He then chose the universe as the means of achieving that, and arranged for the initial conditions for the big bang to lead to that result. What he may have had to do since then, we shall investigate later, but the creatures to which this process has led include you and me.

I am biased towards this viewpoint by other evidence, which atheistic readers will not necessarily accept, but which is, in fact, often the strongest of evidence for believers. That is the evidence of the changes that God makes in the lives of people who accept him. For me, that provides sufficient evidence of the reality of God, though it will not for you unless you experience it for yourself; or unless someone you know well has experienced it, and has changed as a result.

In summary, the arguments underlying the first explanation (that we were lucky in the lottery) are valid, but the second explanation (the intelligent Mind behind the universe) additionally gives a reason as to why the result of the 'lottery' came out as it did. Supporters of the 'we were lucky' view have no explanation as to why it happened like that.

There is another interesting aspect to all of this. As we saw in Chapter Four, our best scientific description of the development of the universe is that it began in a singularity, an almost infinitely dense point of practically zero size. After thinking about an incredibly short period of the universe's early development it becomes clear that the fundamental constants, and the laws of nature which make use of their values, must have been built in 'before' the big bang to give rise to the universe as we now see it. Scientists do use those constants in their investigations of the very early universe, so they have faith that the numbers, and the laws of nature, already existed then.

This effectively then becomes another 'argument from design' for the possible existence of God: the universe seems to have a set of initial constants which were 'already' there at the beginning and which, even if we could understand where their values came from, would still seem to have been designed to lead to conditions favorable to the development of life like us. The same applies to the 'laws of nature' by which the universe works.

This design argument is not susceptible to dismissal in the same way as arguments about the design of the eye, for example. The initial constants and laws of nature did not arise from any kind of gradual evolutionary process that we might, someday, be able to explain. Rather, they were just there. It therefore seems rational that the suggestion that God may have created things just so, is at least as likely as the suggestion that they just happened, with no possibility of any further reason being discovered.

If a fundamental design argument, such as that outlined above, is acceptable, then it does beg the question as to what the purpose of the design was. That purpose was suggested a few paragraphs earlier but, at first sight, it seems far too anthropocentric,[88] and just plain arrogant, to suggest that the entire universe exists so that humans can exist. However, that is not the suggestion being made. The suggestion is only that God intended that some creatures would come to exist, somewhere, who could enter into a loving relationship with him.

Those creatures have turned out to be us, and the place where they exist has turned out to be on Earth, but it is possible that neither of those outcomes was inevitably going to turn out exactly as we see them now. Perhaps the creatures that are capable of relating to God could have turned out to be different from human beings, and the place where they developed could have been elsewhere in the universe.

Perhaps there might be other such worshiping creatures elsewhere in the universe, with their own science, their own revelation from God about his work in the universe, and even their own unnecessary arguments about which of the two views is correct. However, we have no evidence of any kind yet, scientific or religious, for that. In fact, as we shall see, for the conditions to be just right for life, it may be that only a small minority of planets is likely to fit the bill.

Later, we shall revisit the suggestion that God has allowed the universe to make itself in such a way that we came to be where we are. In the meantime, given that the Mind behind the universe intended that self-conscious and worshiping creatures should come to exist, perhaps the only remaining anthropocentric obstacle is the sheer scale of the universe.

Earlier, we saw that we effectively exist on a speck of dust, orbiting a fairly average star, in a somewhat larger than average galaxy, which contains at least 200 billion other stars, and is one of 100 billion galaxies in the observable universe. If there were just our solar system, perhaps it would be more believable that we might be the center of attention – but surely not amongst so many ($10^{22}$) stars?

Maybe it would have to be the way it is though. If you accept the scientific description of the evolution of galaxies and stars, then the universe definitely needs to be of a great age. At least one or two generations of massive stars need to have ended their lives in supernovae, in order to have provided the chemical elements necessary for Earth to exist (Chapter Five).

I have no specialist knowledge as to whether or not a universe of 100 billion galaxies is required in order to provide the necessary conditions for us to exist, but it does seem likely. Every particle in the universe has some gravitational effect on our solar system. The effects of particles on the other side of the universe are so very small that they may seem to be negligible, but gravity is cumulative. The entire mass of the universe, and the effects of dark energy, do therefore affect the behavior of the Milky Way, and hence of The Sun and Earth.

Gravity also affected the early expansion of the universe immediately after the big bang. Then, everything was extremely close together, and hence gravity acted upon the very slight differences in density, so that areas of higher density became denser and areas of lower density became less dense, eventually forming the galaxies, including ours.

If the mass of the universe had been much different, would the fundamental constants have been able to have a different set of values, allowing the universe to form in the same kind of way? We don't know, but, given the fine-tuning we observe, it does seem unlikely. Assuming that the fundamental constants could not be satisfactorily 're-tuned', a different quantity of mass in the early universe would result in a different rate of expansion, stars would not be able to form as they have and there would be catastrophic consequences for the appearance of life, as described in the next chapter.

These are all potentially-significant things for the existence of Earth and, if there is a Mind behind the universe, which desired that creatures with our characteristics should exist, then it is at least conceivable that what we see around us is the result of that Mind instituting the only way it could have been made to happen.

# Chapter 9  A Few Examples of Fine-Tuning

This chapter is mainly taken up with a few specific examples of how finely tuned the universe needs to be, in order for Earth to be able exist as it does, and to be able to support life like us. This is just a fairly random, small selection, simply to confirm that the idea might be significant. There is much more detail in the books referenced in the endnotes.

It is worth pointing out that it is unwise just to look at any one of these examples in isolation. Rather than concentrating on some specific example of fine-tuning, the idea of this chapter is to convey the impression that the whole universe, and everything in it, appears to be the result of some careful design. The alternative view is to accept that the many instances of fine-tuning really are genuine – the evidence is there for all to see – but that we just don't know why.

The first item below should be reasonably easy to follow, though some of the later ones are more technical. Nevertheless, they all contain some potentially interesting comments, putting a few numbers to the degree of fine-tuning required. Our opinion as to the actual values of these numbers may alter, as our understanding of the universe continues to become more refined, but the conclusions probably won't change significantly.

If you find one of the following sections becoming too heavy going for your liking, feel free to skim-read to the next. Do read the last section of the chapter though, as that considers the relationship of all this material to belief in God.

## The Goldilocks zone

We can begin with a fairy tale – yes, it is the only one in the book. You may well be familiar with the tale of Goldilocks. She was the little girl who, to cut a long story short, wandered into the house of three bears. She tried out their chairs, their breakfast porridge and their beds. In every case, those belonging to Mummy and Daddy Bear were at extremes that did not suit her: too hard, too soft, too hot, too cold and so on. However, in each case, the one belonging to Baby Bear was "just right".

In order for life to be able to exist on a planet orbiting a star, its position and characteristics similarly have to be just right. It was back in the 1950s that scientists first realized just how narrow is the zone in which Earth has to orbit The Sun, in order to be able to support life. Technically, this band is called the 'habitable zone' but, popularly, it is often called the 'Goldilocks Zone' because it is just right for life.

All life, as we understand it, is based upon carbon compounds and water. For life to be able to exist on a planet, it is generally agreed that the planet needs to orbit its star in a region where it is neither too hot, nor too cold, for liquid water to exist on its surface.[89]

For any given planetary system around a star, the location of this zone depends upon the amount of thermal radiation emitted by the star; it can be quite narrow. In our solar system, Venus (the next planet from Earth closer to The Sun) is far too hot, partly due to its greenhouse atmosphere, whilst Mars (the next planet from Earth farther away from The Sun) is far too cold.

Many stars actually have no habitable zone at all. There will always be a band at a suitable distance from any star, within which the temperature is such that liquid water would normally be able to exist. However, many stars also emit powerful bursts of radiation, of such intensity that no life could actually survive on a planet in its 'habitable' zone – so it is, in fact, not habitable at all. Farther away from the star, where the sporadic bursts of radiation would be less harmful, a planet would be outside the Goldilocks Zone, and would be too cold for liquid water to exist.

Even on Earth, there is concern amongst scientists and engineers that radiation from certain types of solar flare activity on our own Sun can sometimes disable our communication and electricity distribution systems. This has already happened, and work is in hand to use the prediction of solar flares in temporarily shutting down critical systems on Earth, until a predicted burst of potentially harmful radiation has passed.

Another bad effect in some otherwise-habitable zones around stars is gravitational. You will already know that we only ever see one side of The Moon from Earth. This is due to tidal locking, in which the rotational period of a smaller body, orbiting a larger one, can become locked to be the same as the time it takes the smaller body to orbit the larger one. For a planet orbiting a star, that makes its day the same as its year, so that it rotates on its axis exactly once, as it orbits its star exactly once. The result is that the same face of the smaller body is always facing the larger one, as is the case with The Moon and Earth.

For a planet orbiting a star cooler than The Sun, the habitable zone for its orbit would be nearer to the star than Earth is to The Sun. The planet may then be so near to the star that tidal locking would occur such as that between The Moon and Earth. The same side of the planet would always face the star. There would be no night on one side, and no day on the other. Temperatures would then probably be such that all water would eventually evaporate on the 'day' side, and freeze on the 'night' side, despite the planet theoretically being in a habitable zone. It is conceivable that some kind of life might be able to have a precarious existence in the permanent shadow of a mountain, on the boundary between the permanent day and night hemispheres, but presumably no life as advanced as that on Earth.

Even in the case of Earth, which is not tidally locked, it might only require Earth's orbit to be a few percent nearer to The Sun to mean that oceans would never have formed, or only a few percent farther away to freeze the oceans. It is fairly easy to visualize how delicate our position in the solar system is, by thinking about the extreme regions on Earth where human life is already impossible; at least without the help of a lot of technology. A little nearer to The Sun, and you can easily imagine that there would be more deserts, for example. A little farther away, and there would be more polar ice cap and lower temperatures.

Climate change in Earth's present orbit has already achieved this in the cycles of ice ages over long time periods, so it seems likely that an actual shift in our orbit, one way or the other, would lead to more serious effects.

So, for life requiring water to have any chance of existing on a planet, that planet has to meet the fairly tight requirements for being in the Goldilocks Zone around its star. In addition, it has to be the case that the Goldilocks Zone does not coincide with an area where there are harmful effects either from radiation or from gravity. There are also further restrictions on habitable zones, dependent upon a star's location in its galaxy.

In the case of Earth, The Moon also plays a significant role in stabilizing Earth's rotation. The Moon is very slowly drifting away from Earth. In about a billion years' time, it will be 10 percent further away than it is now. By that time, the reduced influence of The Moon is likely to allow the tilt of Earth's axis to vary significantly from the twenty-three degrees that it is at present.

The tilt of Earth's axis gives rise to our seasons. At present, Earth's polar regions experience day and night for several weeks at a time, in their winters and summers. If the tilt of Earth's axis increases, these periods of extended day and night will lengthen, and will apply to far greater areas of the surface. The temperature difference between day and night will become much more extreme than now, and many animals and plants on Earth will not be able to cope with that, leaving large areas barren. So even Earth, in its Goldilocks zone, relies on The Moon being as large as it is, and positioned pretty much where it is now, in order to sustain life.

In view of considerations such as these, the probability of life elsewhere in the universe is very much lower than that based on simplistic estimates of the likely number of planets. The Kepler Space Telescope[90] identified about 4,600 candidates for planets orbiting other stars in its field of view and, at the time of writing about 1,000 of these had been confirmed by follow-up investigations. However, there are suggestions that only a few of these lie in the habitable zones around their stars and, as we have seen, the 'habitable zone' may not actually be habitable. Then there is still the problem as to how life might arise in any suitable location. After all, we don't yet understand how it arose on Earth. It is therefore a real possibility that we are much lonelier in the universe than some suggest.

## The existence of carbon

In Chapter Five, we looked at the chain of coincidences necessary for the formation of carbon, on which all life, as we know it, is based. Barrow and Tipler, in their huge book, *The Anthropic Cosmological Principle*,[91] describe this as, "A remarkable chain of coincidences", and so it is.

Just to recap very briefly, one coincidence is that the weak nuclear force is sufficiently strong to do its job, but sufficiently weak that stars can have lives long enough to produce carbon at all. Carbon is formed inside stars, by firstly creating a nucleus of beryllium, and then combining a nucleus of helium with it. However, the beryllium nucleus only survives for an extremely short time. The next coincidence is that, given that it is an unstable nucleus, it survives long enough for suitable reactions to occur.

Nevertheless, it would still be too short a time for anything like sufficient carbon to form, were it not for another coincidence. This is the presence of a resonance in the carbon atom that greatly speeds up the reaction, meaning that the short lifetimes of beryllium nuclei are then long enough for the formation of sufficient carbon.

In the normal course of events, all that carbon could then be converted to oxygen in collisions with other helium nuclei. Another coincidence is that a resonance in the oxygen atom, which would have allowed this to happen very easily, turns out to be at just the wrong (or right, for us!) energy level for that to be the case, so that this particular chain of reactions stops at carbon.

Some of the following examples, and others which are not mentioned here, are also coincidences that affect the chain above, so the existence of carbon actually depends on a chain of coincidences even more unlikely than 'only' the four above.

## The forces of gravity and electromagnetism

It is gravity that holds the whole universe together. The attraction between The Moon and Earth is gravitational, and The Moon only stays in orbit, rather than crashing into Earth, because it is moving quite quickly. Conversely, were it not for Earth's gravity balancing The Moon's tendency to escape, it would fly off into space.

Gravity is actually a very weak force though – unless the gravitational effects of a lot of mass accumulate to make it significant in any given situation. For example, Earth's mass is sufficient to cause the gravitational attraction which holds us all onto its surface. However, the gravitational attraction between Earth and me, is 150 billion times greater than that between me and the coffee mug on my desk.

That's why you can't get your coffee simply by holding out your hand and expecting it to slide across the desk to you. There genuinely is a measurable gravitational force of attraction between the mug and you, but it is so tiny that it doesn't even register against the frictional forces resisting the motion of the mug across your desk.

We are fortunate that whatever it is which fixes the force of gravity, has resulted in it being such a weak force. If it was much stronger, everything in the universe could be attracted together and crushed into enormous densities, as neutron stars and black holes have been.

Inside an atom, the gravitational attraction between particles such as protons and electrons is so small that the electromagnetic force completely swamps it. It is therefore not gravity, but the electromagnetic force, attracting electrons to the protons in an atomic nucleus, which balances the energy of motion of the orbiting electrons, and prevents them from flying away from the atom, in the same way as gravity prevents The Moon flying away from Earth.

In his book, *The Goldilocks Enigma*,[30] Paul Davies states that the electromagnetic force is larger than the force of gravity by a factor of about $10^{40}$ (or, if you prefer, 10 thousand trillion trillion trillion). Davies also quotes some previous work by Brandon Carter (the originator of the term 'anthropic principle') in which Carter discovered, by theoretical analysis of certain aspects of stars, that his calculated ratio was, "Very close to the observed value of $10^{40}$." Martin Rees, in his earlier book,[39] gives a somewhat smaller number here, presumably because Davies' number is seven years more up to date. However, Rees does give detailed discussions of several of the bad (for us) consequences, if the relationship between gravity and the electromagnetic force were to differ from whatever it actually is.

Davies also presents some information showing that, "if gravity were a bit stronger ... planets might not form; if gravity were somewhat weaker ... supernovas might never happen." The significance of the latter comment is that, without supernovae, none of the heavier elements would ever have become available to form planets.

There is a balance between the magnitudes of the electromagnetic force and the force of gravity, and both the balance and the actual values need to be pretty near to what we observe them to be, in order for us to be here.

## The strength of the strong nuclear force

A helium atom contains a nucleus comprising two protons and two neutrons. As in all atomic nuclei, these are bound together by the strong nuclear force that acts only over extremely short distances within atomic nuclei.

Nuclear fusion is a very efficient process and, as a result, in the case of the reactions that convert hydrogen to helium, the mass of the resulting helium atom is 99.3% of the mass of the protons and neutrons that were used in its construction. Thus, according to Rees,[39] only 0.7%, that is a proportion of 0.007, of the original nuclear mass, is radiated away as heat.

Rees explains that, if this number had been 0.006 rather than 0.007, then the strong nuclear force would be too weak to bind a proton to a neutron, so helium would not be able to form. Therefore, neither would any heavier elements; the universe would only contain hydrogen, so there would be no Earth and no life.

On the other hand, if the number exceeded 0.008, then the strong nuclear force would be so strong that two protons (a hydrogen nucleus is a proton) could be bound together directly, irrespective of the electrical repulsion due to their positive charges, whereas, as things are, extra mass from the neutrons is required. The conditions believed to have existed in the big bang were such that, had the number exceeded 0.008, no hydrogen would have been left to fuel stars.

Had there been no stars, no solar systems could exist, and hence no life. This number therefore has to be somewhere near the center of the range 0.006 to 0.008 to make life possible. Again, science cannot tell us why the value is (say) 0.007, rather than (say) 0.005 but, if it were not, we wouldn't be here.

## Dark matter and dark energy

This section includes what Paul Davies describes as "the biggest fix in the universe" – it is the most extreme fine-tuning example of which I am aware.

It has been known for many years that the density of matter in the very early universe (the number of kilograms of mass in each cubic meter of space) was crucial to the subsequent evolution of the universe.

If the universe had been a little denser than it was, the gravitational attraction between all the particles of mass in the universe would soon have overcome the outward expansion of the big bang. The expansion would have been brought to a halt and then the universe would have re-collapsed, so we would not be here.

Conversely, if the density had been a little lower, the gravitational attraction opposing the expansion would have been lower, so the expansion would have been more rapid than it has been. In that case, matter could have flown apart too rapidly to allow time for stars to form and, again, we would not be here.

There is a critical figure for the density of the universe, which marks the boundary between a universe that will expand forever, and one that will stop expanding and then collapse. Given that the universe is now about 13.7 billion years old, in order for the density of the universe to be as it is today, the initial density must have been very close indeed to that critical value. Otherwise, over the great age of the universe, the separation of the galaxies would, by now, have become either very much greater, or very much smaller, than it actually is.

However, as our knowledge has increased, things have become less straightforward. In addition to the matter which we can see in the universe because it is in shining stars, there is a large amount of 'dark matter', so-called because, unsurprisingly, we can't see it. There is no reason why most of the matter in the visible universe should have formed itself into bright stars and, in fact, it now seems that a large proportion of the matter in the universe is dark.

The presence of some of the matter that we cannot see can be inferred by its effects on the behavior of stars, galaxies and clusters of galaxies that we *can* see. For example, many stars have been found to wobble slightly in the sky and this has been deduced to be due to the presence of a dark companion star orbiting, as a 'binary system' with the bright star, around their shared center of mass.[92]

In 1998, a strange discovery was made – the rate of expansion of the universe is actually increasing. To appreciate why this is strange, imagine throwing a ball. After the ball has left your hand, it is always going to be slowing down due to frictional drag from the air. The only way to make the ball accelerate in mid-flight would be somehow to give it an extra push by imparting some extra energy to it. In the same way, if the expansion of the universe is accelerating, this must be due to the input of some extra energy, after the initial big bang.

The extra energy required to account for the accelerating expansion of the universe has been named 'dark energy'. Its effect now suggests that the universe will expand indefinitely.

It is now believed that this dark energy must contribute about 73 percent of the entire mass-energy of the universe, but nobody yet knows where it comes from, or how it exercises its 'anti-gravity' effect upon the matter in the universe. One suggestion is that, in the 'empty' space between stars and galaxies, there could be 'vacuum energy' arising from the chance quantum fluctuations that are believed to occur all the time and everywhere. As Stephen Hawking says in *The Universe in a Nutshell*,[93] "Remarkably enough, the effect of vacuum energy is the opposite of that of matter ... vacuum energy causes the expansion [of the universe] to accelerate."

It seems that this extra force due to dark energy must only become significant in interstellar space, and that it has no discernible effect over distances of less than one billion light-years. If its effect was not so small, it would have pushed matter apart more rapidly, prevented stars from forming and, again, there would then have been no life in the universe. But how small is "small" in this case?

In the early 20th century, Albert Einstein introduced a 'cosmological constant' into his relativity equations. This constant is now effectively used to model the acceleration of the expansion of the universe due to the dark energy (though that was not Einstein's original purpose[94]).

The intriguing thing is that the required effect of the cosmological constant is almost unbelievably small. Davies[30] gives a fairly detailed description of the thinking on dark energy, and describes how cosmologists predicted the likely density of dark energy from considerations of quantum theory; the result was astonishingly large. However, at that time, physicists believed that the actual effects due to dark energy were zero.

Given that precisely zero was thought to be required, the scientists were almost prepared to accept that some mechanism, as yet unknown, must exactly cancel out the effects predicted by quantum theory. However, when the rate of expansion of the universe was found to be increasing, that indicated that the effects of dark energy were not actually zero after all, since they are thought to be responsible for the accelerating expansion.

I can't go into the detail here, but in what Davies describes as perhaps the "biggest fix in the universe", this requires the previously described "astonishingly large" number, to be not quite cancelled out. Nevertheless, the cancellation does need to be complete to the tune of one part in $10^{120}$. That is the largest number in this book, and the cancellation to one part in $10^{120}$ leaves the smallest number in the book. To all normal intents and purposes, the result is zero (0.00000...one hundred and ten more zeros...00001), but here, it is important that it is not *exactly* zero.

Davies compares the odds of obtaining such a level of almost-but-not-quite cancellation, with trying to flip consecutive 'heads' when flipping a coin. He points out that it is, "Like getting heads no fewer than *400 times in a row* [Davies' italics]." For comparison, odds of one-in-a-million are equivalent to flipping 'only' 20 consecutive heads. Davies also says, "The cliché that 'life is balanced on a knife edge' is a staggering understatement in this case: no knife in the universe could have an edge *that* fine [Davies' italics]." As he points out, if the results were not as described above, against odds equivalent to flipping 400 consecutive heads, then we wouldn't be here.

## The smoothness of the universe

Earlier, we mentioned the tiny density fluctuations in the very early universe, which eventually gave rise to the galaxies, and clusters of galaxies, which we now observe. The equivalent degree of smoothness would be an Earth whose highest mountain is only a few meters high.

If the matter in the big bang had been exactly uniformly distributed (completely 'smooth'), then the expansion of the universe would have led to equal densities of matter everywhere. The universe would still be a uniformly distributed sea of hydrogen and helium, with no stars and no life.

If the density fluctuations in the very early universe had been much larger than one part in 100,000, the concentration of mass into 'clumps', as the universe expanded, would have happened more rapidly. There would now be fewer groupings of mass than the number of galaxies that we actually see, and each of them would, on average, contain much more mass than the galaxies do now.

That would be a problem, because such super-dense galaxies would tend to collapse under gravity more rapidly than actual galaxies do. Stars would be much closer together, and would tear each other apart gravitationally. Stable planetary systems would not be possible, as they would also be disrupted by the gravitational attraction of nearby stars. Again, there would therefore be no life.

One measure of how tightly objects are bound together by gravity, is the amount of energy it would take to separate them, compared with their total 'rest mass energy', which can be found from Einstein's famous equation $E=mc^2$.

According to Rees,[39] it appears that it would take only a factor of about $10^{-5}$ (one thousandth of one percent) of the rest mass energy of the largest structures in the universe (clusters and super clusters of galaxies) to disrupt them. This factor is sufficiently greater than zero to allow galaxies of just the correct sort of densities for life to appear out of an almost featureless initial universe. If it had been much larger, then, as Rees says, "The universe would have been a violent place, in which no stars or solar systems could survive."

## The masses of the proton and neutron

The proton and neutron are both extremely small, sub-atomic particles, which make up the nuclei of atoms, but they do have some mass. It turns out that the neutron is about 0.14 percent heavier than the proton.

Paul Davies[30] points out that this is extremely important for the nuclear physics which goes on within stars, but particularly, that if the neutron was lighter by a fraction of one percent, it would then be lighter than the proton. The consequences of that would have been that, "Isolated protons, rather than neutrons ... would be unstable. Then ... without protons there could be no atoms and no chemistry." And, of course, no life.

## What can we conclude from this?

If you have read even one or two of the items in this chapter, you have probably realized that our existence in the universe really hangs by a thread, which, in turn, hangs by another thread, and so on. It really does seem highly improbable. Most people would agree with that, but the question is, what should we make of it?

Many other examples of fine-tuning could be quoted, including some from other fields such as chemistry where, for example, it is surprising just how perfectly fitted are the properties of water for life. That is precisely why the possibility of the existence of liquid water is used as the indicator of the habitable zone around a star.

Given all the examples that could be mustered, it is then tempting to conclude that God must therefore exist, because it is all just too improbable to have happened by chance. That is actually what I think, but I am aware of some pitfalls.

One of these is that religious people do tend to select one example of fine-tuning and point out that, if some number or other had been slightly different from what it actually is, we should not be here. Most of the sections above, if taken in isolation, look exactly like that.

The more cautious view is that perhaps one of the numbers actually could be different, but that there could still be a universe supporting life if some of the other numbers were simultaneously also changed to new values. In other words, we should not put too much emphasis on changes in individual parameters governing the behavior of the universe, as they all interact.

Some supporters of fine-tuning as evidence for God, say that it is highly unlikely that any set of fundamental parameters of the universe other than the set we have, could work. Opponents suggest otherwise. Neither has a watertight case though, as we simply don't know enough about how all these variables interact in such a complex system.

In my field of control systems, if a system has a well-tuned performance, using a very common type of controller that has three adjustable parameters, then changing the value of any one of the three parameters will adversely affect the performance of the system. However, if the other two parameters are then re-tuned, the previous level of performance can sometimes be regained, now with a different set of three parameters from the original set. This is not always the case though, even with only three tunable values.

In more complex control systems, it is often not at all clear how the previous performance can be regained after varying one of the control parameters, or even whether it is possible to regain it at all. If that is the case when re-tuning an industrial control system, which must surely be exceedingly straightforward when compared with tuning a universe, the difficulties involved in re-tuning the universe must be huge.

Even if science, one day, manages to explain all the numerical values we have mentioned, together with many others, and also manages to explain their required degree of precision, it still begs the question as to why all that information was imprinted in the universe right at the start. I will still be able to say that it was because the Mind of God conceived a universe such as ours, and tuned it accordingly.

## Chapter 10  Free Will and Free World

Many religious people believe that God was responsible for setting up the initial conditions for the big bang at the beginning of everything. Many also believe that he is still active in sustaining the universe, that he answers prayers, and that he acts in people's lives. A problem then arises though, namely that scientists need to be able to rely on their faith in the regularity and consistency of the behavior of the universe since, without those, any results of science would be unreliable.

If God is active in the universe, particularly on Earth as far as we are concerned, should we perhaps expect miracles to be happening all the time and everywhere? If they did, surely that would then lead to a lot of random behavior, destroying the consistency and regularity which we actually observe, and removing the scientists' ability to apply the scientific method, or to make any reliable discoveries or predictions.

Also, if God is still active in the universe, should we perhaps expect all our prayers to be granted? If they were, that would have the same effect – tending to randomize the behavior of the world. In the film *Bruce Almighty*, Bruce Nolan complains about the way in which God is running the world and, as a result, ends up being given some of God's powers to see if he can do any better. When clicking through a list of prayer requests on his computer system, he gets fed up of considering them all one by one and decides to click the "Yes to all" button. Chaos ensues. As just one example, everyone wins the lottery, but that means that the prizes are tiny, and there are riots in the streets.

If God does act in response to the prayers of humans, especially in obviously miraculous ways, how is it that the behavior of the world remains so regular and consistent? This chapter suggests a way in which these seemingly contradictory ideas can fit together and, as a result, how that might help us with the answers to any other difficult questions about the way the world seems to be, such as the perennial problem of pain and suffering.

Some of the ideas in this chapter may prove controversial for some readers; indeed, I am not completely happy with all the consequences that follow from them. Nevertheless, they do seem to give the best explanation of the way things seem to be. The other choices are either to propose an alternative rational explanation that fits the facts as well as the ideas below, or simply to abandon the attempt.

One rational alternative would be atheism, but that seems to leave us short of satisfactory answers to many of the ultimate 'why' questions; it also leaves us short of answers as to where values, morals, purpose, beauty, truth, meaning, and worship come from. It offers little in the way of hope to those who are suffering or dying, and it sets aside as meaningless the very real experiences of God enjoyed by many generations of people.

Another alternative is simply to say that we can't understand how God can act in the world, but he does; so we rely on faith without much thought. Assuming that God exists, he must be far more powerful, wise and knowledgeable than we are, so it is true that we cannot ultimately expect to be able to understand everything which he might do, or allow. However, to someone with an inquiring mind, it does seem to be intellectually lazy not to try our best to understand, though there will be limits, as the following story illustrates.

We have a pet cat. Sometimes, she might think (had her brain evolved sufficiently) that she is made to suffer for our amusement. For example, sometimes she is denied any food in the morning, even though she whines for it. She is then caught and forced into a box, which she doesn't like. Then she is taken for a ride in a car, which she hates because it always makes her ill. Then someone spends a few minutes poking her about and sticking needles into her, before she gets another bad car trip back home.

She would be justified in believing that she is being tortured for fun – after all, what other reason could there possibly be? But that is because she understands nothing of the diseases she could catch, the unpleasant and potentially fatal effects that they could have, and the work a vet has to do to prevent them.

Actually, of course, it is all for the cat's benefit – she needs regular check-ups and injections to keep her healthy. The alternative could be far, far worse. We know that the cat hates her trips to the vet, and we know that she genuinely does suffer. In fact, those trips upset my wife almost as much as they upset the cat. However, we also know that it is the very best we can do for the cat in the long run.

Furthermore, we do minimize her suffering as much as we can; hence the lack of breakfast, since we know that any food she eats is all going to come back later. The cat, on the other hand, probably doesn't even know that there is a "later"! The bad things that we do to the cat are the 'dark side' of her leading a healthier life than she otherwise would.

There is no way that the cat can understand any of this. Our levels of wisdom and knowledge are far greater than those of a cat. Our self-consciousness and our thinking are on a completely different level, totally inaccessible to the cat. That is why we understand what is happening to the cat, the suffering it causes, and the reasons why it has to happen, but the cat doesn't.

However, that difference must pale into insignificance when compared with the difference in the level of wisdom and knowledge between a perfect God, and us. Can we therefore expect to make sense of all the bad things that happen to us? We can go much farther than a cat can but, compared with the wisdom and knowledge of God, the answer, in the end, is no.

One morning the cat gets breakfast, the next she doesn't. She can't see any difference whatsoever between the two occasions, and therefore can't understand why she gets no food on the second occasion, but we know that the cat needs to go to the see the vet that morning. Similarly, God might well need to act very differently in two situations that, to us, may seem identical.

According to the Bible, Jesus was once asked, "What is the greatest commandment?" He replied, "Love the Lord your God with all your heart and with all your soul and with all your mind and with all your strength." [95] The reference to "mind" suggests that, if we have been blessed with inquiring minds, then we should think things out as far as we are able. Then we can understand God better and love him more. That was the impulse which motivated many of the founders of modern science to try to understand the universe, and still motivates many today.

God is accessible to everyone, no matter at what level they are capable of understanding him, or how they choose to engage with him. But, if you are capable of making that choice, you do need positively to choose to engage with him, once you become aware of that possibility. If we have sufficient mental capacity to exercise our free will in that respect, then God will honor our choice, whether we choose to follow him, or choose to go our own way.

If someone, through force of circumstance, never receives the appropriate information on which to base such a choice, or doesn't have the mental capacity to choose, then because God is loving, just and fair, we can safely entrust all such people to him.

We need to be very careful though, and very open to correction, when suggesting what our human understanding of God seems to commit him to. The same kind of humility should apply if we propose that there is no god at all since, as we saw earlier, there is no definitive proof of that.

## What does God have to do with free will?

Whilst some philosophers continue to argue over whether or not we have free will, I am convinced that I have the freedom to choose what I will do. A little while ago, I went downstairs to the kitchen and made a drink. I am sure that I didn't *have* to do that. I thought about it for a moment, in a shall-I-shan't-I sort of way, and *chose* to do it, on the basis that the result of doing it was preferable to the result of not doing it.

That choice could have had consequences though, even though it was something so trivial. Maybe I could have slipped on the stairs and broken my neck, which would not have happened had I stayed at my desk in the study. Maybe, if I had stayed at my desk, the large oak tree outside might have been blown down, come through the roof and hit me, which I would have avoided by going downstairs.

Every time we are faced with a decision in which a choice has to be made, I feel that we are free to make the choice for ourselves, but that there will be consequences, whichever way we choose.

Many choices are much more important than a decision to break off from writing for a couple of minutes. Should you apply for a particular job? Should you leave a job (if you are fortunate enough to have one)? Should you study for a particular qualification? Should you marry a particular person? Should you move to live in a different area? Where should your children go to school? If you are fortunate enough to have some money, should you spend a large proportion of it on some particular item?

These choices have obvious consequences, but also some which may be less obvious. For example, if you change jobs, or move to a different area, you will also change the set of people you know. Some of the new people you meet may have significant effects on the course of the rest of your life, which will soon be very different from what it would otherwise have been.

You will immediately find yourself in a different set of circumstances from before, with different outcomes, and leading your life in a different direction. You may meet with an accident because your new circumstances put you in a certain place at a certain time. Alternatively, you may avoid meeting certain people, or having an accident, because of no longer being in the other place and time of your previous circumstances.

The interactions between the everyday choices we make, and the similar choices being made, all the time, by everyone else, are obviously very complex. But the fact is that the choices we all make, even seemingly trivial ones, might have consequences that can affect the rest of our lives, and the lives of others with whom we subsequently come into contact. This even applies to something as simple as deciding to catch a later train, rather than an earlier one. You can easily imagine some possibly far-reaching consequences, both good and bad, of doing that.

Wearing my Christian hat, the reason we have the free will to make choices is that God wants us to have meaningful relationships with him. In fact, his greatest wish is for us to choose to love him, as indicated by the verse from Mark's gospel, quoted in the previous section.[95]

The word *choose* is important here. You cannot *make* someone love you; it has to be their choice. Perhaps the best explanation here is that God has chosen to allow that to be true of his relationship with us; he cannot force us to 'love' him, but he has allowed us free will so that we can genuinely love him, having freely chosen to do so. At the same time, we have no difficulty in getting God to love us. He loves you and me more than anyone else could, because he created the universe so that creatures would exist who could choose to love him. He is always ready for a relationship with us.

I am not suggesting that God knew, when he set up the conditions for the early universe, that a particular (or indeed any) human being would one day exist, who would be known as Ken Dutton, and that he would write this book. If that concerns you, because you believe that God must know all the details of everything, please reserve judgment until the end of the book before writing me off as a heretic.

Perhaps we could have been created like robots, with no free will, programmed to love God. But what would be the point in that? If someone *had* to love you, with no choice in the matter, such 'love' would be both meaningless and worthless.

It has often been pointed out that, from God's point of view, allowing us free will was a tremendous risk. Having given us the choice as to whether to love him or not, the risk was that we would not. Many of us don't; even many of us who do, don't love him as much as we should. That seems to leave God with a problem.

From the viewpoint of Christianity, the ways in which we should behave have been revealed in the life of Jesus Christ, in the Bible, and by many centuries of interpretation of it. Also, as we saw in Chapter Seven, God seems to have placed a 'moral law' inside us, which tells us what is right and wrong, independently of our culture.

If, in spite of all these things, we choose to oppose God, then because he has given us that free choice there will be a limit to how often (if at all) he can overrule the free choice which he has given, whilst remaining a faithful and reliable God worthy of our love.

It seems that this has to be the case if God is consistent and reliable. He won't give us free will with one hand, and arbitrarily take it away with the other. C.S. Lewis, in his book, *The Problem Of Pain*, gave short shrift to people who are prone to claim that God can do both of two mutually exclusive things. He wrote, "If you choose to say 'God can give a creature free will and at the same time withhold free will from it', you have not succeeded in saying *anything* about God: meaningless combinations of words do not suddenly acquire meaning simply because we prefix them with two other words 'God can' ... nonsense remains nonsense even when we talk it about God [Lewis' italics]." [83]

Our abuse of the free will that God allows us also explains some of the problems in the world. For example, a lot of suffering is caused by humans failing to follow God's way of love. The majority of wars, refugee crises, terrorism, mal-nourishment and lack of sanitation and medication in the third world, preventable illness which is allowed to happen, family breakdown, crime, vandalism and so on, can ultimately be traced back to human ambition, greed and selfishness of one kind or another. In the end, ambition and greed usually stem from selfishness. All such problems therefore result from putting our wishes before God's.

Perhaps we could also add to this category such things as the suffering caused by climatic changes due to human misuse of Earth's resources, or illnesses caused by unnatural diets, smoking, drugs or alcohol.

The actions of tyrants such as Idi Amin, Hitler, Mao Tse Tung, Pol Pot and Stalin may have to be allowed to take place, if such people have chosen so to exercise their God-given free will, even if it is against the wishes of God. The fault, though, lies with the perpetrators, not with God.

I subscribe to the idea that, by giving us free will, God has deliberately chosen to limit his power to force humans to take certain courses of action. Even if you accept that idea though, the extent to which such a limitation might apply raises interesting questions. For example, can God *never* overrule someone's free will? If he sometimes can, why didn't he do so in cases such as the atrocities committed by the dictators mentioned above, which resulted in millions of unnecessary deaths?

Thinking back to the suffering of our cat, described earlier, two situations that seem identical to us might look very different from God's viewpoint, because of his much wider knowledge of all the considerations that might apply. In that case, although it may seem unacceptable to us, God's best course of action may be very different in the two cases. Perhaps God has averted some instances of genocide but, for whatever reason, could not do so in these cases.

A more straightforward explanation would be that God remains consistent and never overrules anyone's free will. Some ideas as to how he might, nevertheless, still be able to act in people's lives, even those who don't know him, and even including people like the dictators mentioned above, will be suggested later.

## Does the universe make itself?

In my church there is a certain song that we often sing, about the majesty and power of God as demonstrated in creation. On the whole it is an excellent song, but one line suggests that God has told every lightning bolt where it should go. Whenever we sing that line, I can't help but look around at the people present, and wonder what someone will make of it if their house has been struck by lightning.

The line in the song is presumably poetic language, intended only to illustrate the kind of power that God has, and not to be taken literally. If it were to be taken literally though you can, no doubt, appreciate the problem.

There is a serious question here though, namely, if God is in charge of nature, and if he is all-loving, why would he send a lightning bolt to destroy the place where someone lives, possibly causing injury or death in addition to the potential loss of their home? Similarly, why would he cause a volcanic eruption, or an earthquake, perhaps followed by a tsunami?

Some people build such things into arguments against the existence of God. Others simply shrug their shoulders and say that we can't hope to understand why God either actively causes such things, or passively allows them to happen.

Even in the twenty first century, some people might still be tempted to claim that a lightning strike on a building was God's judgment on somebody who lived there, and a warning to the rest of us to toe the line. That's a very last-millennium viewpoint though. It would mean that God is vindictive, which is not in accord with the overview of God's nature as it is revealed in the life and teachings of Jesus. It also seems a remarkably counter-productive tactic for God to use, in attempting to persuade people to love him.

Based upon my understanding of the nature of God, he would not deliberately send a lightning bolt to strike number 666, Providence Avenue, and wreck the lives of the innocent people within. Similarly he would not deliberately cause other natural disasters, knowing that many innocent people would suffer as a result.

Instead, in a similar way to that in which God may have chosen to restrict himself (to some degree) by giving people free will, it makes sense to suggest that he might also have chosen to restrict his actions (to some degree) in the natural world; hence the latter part of the title of this chapter.

This is a more controversial idea than the free-will discussion. One reason for this is that many people also believe that God still acts in the world, both to uphold creation as a whole, and sometimes in more surprising ways. We then have to wonder what God may, or may not, be able to do and that, in turn, means that 'omnipotent' (that is, 'all-powerful') needs defining carefully, when we apply it to God.

Recall some of the suggestions from earlier chapters: that the big bang was God's chosen method of bringing the universe into being; that genetic mutation and natural selection comprise, at least to some extent, his chosen method of allowing species of life to develop; but also that God still acts in the universe today.

So perhaps God largely allows the universe to make itself, but it isn't completely left to run like clockwork. That will cause us some difficulties, but they are no greater than the difficulties of any other approach to problems such as natural disasters and suffering, and this idea seems to give the explanation which best matches reality, and a consistent idea of God.

So, where does this idea come from? No doubt there are medieval, or earlier, versions of it,[96] but the 'modern' version dates from the mid nineteenth century.

When Charles Darwin published his ideas about natural selection, in *On The Origin Of Species* in 1859, not all religious people were dismayed by it. Some high-profile churchmen, for example, realized that Darwin's ideas might explain how God had arranged for living things to evolve from other living things; though not where living things came from in the first place.

The churchmen in question included Frederick Temple, who was an Anglican clergyman, later to become Archbishop of Canterbury, and also Charles Kingsley. Kingsley had been an Anglican rector, and then became Professor of Modern History at Cambridge. He was also a keen naturalist, and the author of several well-known books.

According to John Polkinghorne, "In words used by both Charles Kingsley and Frederick Temple in the aftermath of the publication of the *Origin*, an evolving world may appropriately be thought of theologically as a creation in which creatures are 'allowed to make themselves'." [97]

In Polkinghorne's book *Science And Creation*,[98] he quotes Charles Darwin as follows: in the second edition of *On The Origin Of Species*, Darwin reported that a "celebrated author and divine" had written to him saying, "I have gradually learnt to see that it is as noble a conception of the Deity to believe that He created a few original forms capable of self-development into other and needful forms, as to believe that He required a fresh act of creation to supply the voids caused by the actions of His laws."

For what it's worth, Darwin's "celebrated author and divine" may have been the aforementioned Charles Kingsley.[99] Alister McGrath, in his book *A Fine-Tuned Universe*,[100] also gives a relevant quotation from a sermon of Charles Kingsley's: "We knew of old that God was so wise that He could make all things: but behold, He is so much wiser than even that, that He can make all things make themselves."

Polkinghorne calls this a "free process" argument, drawing a parallel between the "free will" argument for humans, and processes that are free to follow the natural laws in the behavior of the universe. He has explained the idea further in several of his books; in *Quarks Chaos and Christianity*,[20] for example, he says, "Cosmic history is not the unfolding of an inexorable divine plan. An evolutionary world is to be understood theologically as a world allowed by the Creator to make itself to a large degree ... creation is not the starting off of something that is produced ready-made; rather it is a *continuous process* [Polkinghorne's italics]."

As to what this might mean in practice, in chapters four and five we have already seen, in fairly broad-brush terms, how science believes the fabric of the universe to have evolved since the big bang. It has interesting parallels with the 'chance and necessity' involved in the evolution of life on Earth as outlined in Chapter Six.

The randomness of tiny fluctuations in the density of the very early universe, leading to the formation of the galaxies, is mirrored by the randomness of genetic mutation. The regular physics of the formation of galaxies and stars, and of the nuclear reactions within those stars, is mirrored by the regular processes by which evolution proceeds on Earth.

Observations of the universe fit the big bang theory extremely well, and that theory has also successfully predicted some things that were unknown at the time, but were later found to be true. This is a theory of the evolution of the universe that is, therefore, very widely accepted by scientists.

There is apparently no need for God in this description of creation following the big bang. The scientific description seems to explain, fairly comprehensively, what has occurred. There are however, some things for which God is required, if a full description of the universe is the aim.

These include the fact that the finely tuned initial conditions, and the required laws of nature which science is still discovering, were built in 'before' the beginning; the cause of the big bang itself; and the reliability, consistency and apparent universality of the laws of nature. I think that God is the explanation for matters such as these, and also the answer to Leibnitz's famous question, "Why is there something, rather than nothing". I also believe that God has arranged things so that the "something" is understandable by us.

Similarly, in the evolution of life, there seems no need to invoke God where science can (or may, eventually) satisfactorily explain things. This is not a competition. In fact, given some of the unpleasant things that have evolved, it is sometimes perhaps for the best if God is not invoked! [101]

Since science still has little idea as to how the first life appeared on Earth, you may take the view that God directly caused it and that evolution could then proceed from there. Also, since science still does not understand consciousness, you might take the view that God directly implanted it into higher animals. The same applies to the self-consciousness experienced by humans, and a few of the higher animals.

Perhaps you might also think that God directly caused the unimaginable leap in brainpower which allowed humans to develop agriculture, art, commerce, education, engineering, language, literature, mathematics, medicine, music, philosophy, religion, science, and so on. Humans carry out all these things to a degree totally eclipsing all other species' 'achievements'. Many of those areas have not even been 'attempted' by other species at all.

Personally, I remain wary of the 'god of the gaps' trap eventually catching out those who hold such beliefs. However, it wouldn't at all surprise me if God were directly responsible at least for originating life and self-consciousness – but I wouldn't pin my faith on it.

There is an intriguing (though by no means mainstream) suggestion in the area of self-consciousness, and consciousness of God, which runs something like this. Imagine two gases being mixed to make a flammable mixture, hydrogen and air for example. Air, fortunately for us, doesn't burn. However, hydrogen doesn't burn either, unless it is mixed with oxygen. Starting with pure hydrogen, and gradually adding more air (which contains the required oxygen), there comes a very definite hydrogen:air ratio at which the mixture will burn. After that specific point, the behavior of the mixture, in the presence of a spark, is utterly different; it explodes, rather than not burning at all.

If the theory of evolution seems sound, but you would still like to be able to believe in the existence of an original pair of modern humans called, for the sake of argument, Adam and Eve, here's a way it might be possible.

Presumably, as humans evolved, our brains gradually developed. In the same way as there comes a definite point at which the hydrogen and air mixture will burn, at some stage, perhaps there came a definite level of brain evolution at which humans would be able to accept the idea of God, and the way that he would like them to behave. Just maybe, at that time, God selected a likely couple of humans, let's call them Adam and Eve, and showed them how they could have a relationship with him.[102]

Interestingly, it is thought that the DNA in the mitochondria of human cells (Chapter Six) is passed on only from the female parent in every case. Tracing mutations in this DNA backwards indicates that all humans who are alive today may be descended from a single female ancestor, sometimes called "Mitochondrial Eve".[103] Maybe the idea of God 'interfering' in the lives of two early humans could also explain this. But back to the story...

Setting aside such speculations, even if science does eventually remove the need to invoke God to cause the first life to appear from inanimate chemicals, and even if it does also eventually explain the workings of the human brain, for reasons given earlier it would still be possible to claim that God allowed the universe to make itself in such a way that we have evolved as we have.

But was the universe perhaps wound up by a god who then simply sat back to let it run its own course, without taking any further part in the proceedings? I don't think so, and the next chapter considers how God might still act in the world today.

As an introduction to that, over the last few millennia billions of very intelligent people have claimed that they have had an encounter with God. They have claimed that God has affected their lives, and those of their friends; they have claimed that he has answered prayers.

If just one of those billions of such people is correct in any such claim, then God exists and is still active in the universe. Conversely, if no god is active in the universe, then every single one of those billions of people has been wrong. That is, of course, a possibility; a large body of favorable opinion doesn't necessarily make something true.

After all, there have also been large numbers of people who have denied the existence of any god down the ages, though their numbers are presumably far fewer than the numbers of believers, based on the tendency of every civilization to worship gods of some kind. However, in the case of those who do claim encounters with God, there is also weight of personal experience, in addition to mere opinion, which is unavailable to those who claim that there is no god.

It seems highly improbable that every single one of those billions of people who have believed that they have experienced something of God in their lives, has been completely wrong about it. It is often said that there is a God-shaped hole in the center of each of us, which is never satisfactorily filled by worldly things such as fame, human relationships, money, possessions, success or vocations; quite so.

The view that God wound up the universe, set it going, and then effectively retired from the scene to sit back and watch, having no interaction with his creation, is preferred by some scientists who want to believe in the existence of God. It removes any need to think about how God might be able to act, in a day-to-day way, without it being very obvious, and without it removing the reliability of the way the world works, on which science completely relies.

By definition though, nobody who holds that kind of view has had any kind of encounter with God. If God doesn't act in the world, then he cannot have encounters with people.

Conversely, if God does have encounters with people, then he does act in the world. Any encounter with God is likely to change a person's behavior, and therefore to change the future interactions of that person with others and with the world. If God acts in that way, then perhaps he can act in other ways too. I believe that there is such interaction between God and the world. How much interaction is an interesting question though, which is introduced in the next chapter.

On a more theological note, there are also various verses in the Bible that do suggest that the creative work of God, at least as understood by those of the Jewish and Christian faiths, is a continuous work. This is not the place for a bible study but, if you are interested, one or two such references appear in this endnote.[104]

At the very simplest, if the universe only exists because God willed it to, then presumably it only continues to exist because he wills it to. He could decide, at any moment, that it should end. In that sense, at least, his creative action is therefore continuing today. The next chapter looks at more direct kinds of action.

# Chapter 11  Does God Act in the World?

The previous chapter suggested that God has given us free will, and will not therefore overrule it too often (if at all); and that he has allowed creation to make itself, and will not therefore interfere with that too often (if at all). This may seem to leave God with a problem.

Keith Ward sums up this problem nicely, at the beginning of his book *Divine Action*,[105] when he says, "It often seems that we can neither stand the thought of God acting often (since that would infringe our freedom), nor the thought of him acting rarely (since that makes him responsible for our suffering)."

I would add that if God were to act too often in an obvious kind of way, it would also cause much randomness in the world; perhaps too much for science to be able to function. Science relies on finding repeatable patterns of behavior in the universe in order to discover and test its laws. If God had caused too many unpredictable changes in the behavior of the universe, how could we have come to understand its workings so well?

So, what might God still be able to do? We begin with a fairly straightforward comment on prayer.

## Prayer

An honest atheist will never pray, since she has faith in the belief that there is no God to hear her. A non-religious person, who wouldn't go so far as to call himself an atheist, might pray occasionally. However, he is probably only going to turn to prayer as a last resort, in the vague hope that it might achieve something when there seems to be no other way. Such a person probably views prayer purely as a means of asking for something; and then probably only for himself, or those very close to him.

For religious people, prayer is communicating with God, and that communication may take several forms, and have several purposes. It may be to express our love for him, our gratitude to him and our worship of him. It is also a way by which God can speak into our lives, and, yes, it is also a way of asking him to intervene to help others or relieve bad situations.

If you take on board the theology outlined in this book, there is no problem with communicating with God, expressing love for him, worshiping him and receiving from him. However, what might happen when we ask him to act directly in the world is less straightforward.

For example, suppose I discover that someone is about to carry out an evil action, and I pray that she might be restrained from doing so. God may not be able to answer that prayer, because he has already granted her the free will that allows her to choose to do the evil action.

Alternatively, perhaps I might pray that God would arrange for some information to be put in that person's way, or a thought to be put into her head, which would give her another opportunity to reconsider her evil intention, so that she might then freely choose not to carry it out.

The difference may seem subtle, but it is real. If the person does not carry out the evil act, then either of the prayers can be deemed to have succeeded. However, if she does carry it out, the conclusion to be drawn differs, depending on which prayer was prayed.

If I prayed that God would restrain the person from her evil act, then my prayer has not been answered. Perhaps God will not directly restrain someone, if he has given her free will. However, if I prayed that God would give her extra information that might allow her to reconsider her free choice, it is quite likely that God did so (since he would not wish an evil act to be carried out), but that she still exercised her free will, and carried out the evil act anyway. This prayer was answered, even though the outcome was not the one for which I had hoped.

I am not suggesting for a moment that we must always choose our words with great care if we want our prayers to be answered. God knows our hearts and our real desires, however naively we may phrase them, which is why the prayer of a little child can be just as effective as that of a professional theologian.

I'm sure that God is never pedantic in such a situation; surely he would interpret the first prayer as implying the second, if the second is the way in which he can work. The person who prays such prayers may be needlessly discouraged though, if the first of the two approaches is used.

In the same vein, there is little point in praying for no earthquakes to happen, and no volcanoes to erupt, if those things are results of the way in which God has allowed creation to make itself. So far as we can tell, they are a necessary part of recycling Earth's resources. Also, they are unavoidable by-products of Earth's having a molten outer-core of iron and nickel. If Earth didn't have that molten core, we should be in real trouble, as we shall see.

One speculative suggestion is that life originated around thermal vents on the ocean floor. That may, or may not, be the case but, if it is true, we would not be here were it not for those heat sources deep within our planet.

A much more definite discovery is that currents in Earth's molten outer core are responsible for generating Earth's magnetic field. That field spreads far into space, and is responsible for shielding us from much of the potentially harmful radiation from The Sun. If Earth didn't have a molten core, the magnetic field would be absent, and we could not survive the full onslaught of The Sun's radiation. However, the unfortunate 'dark side' of the molten core is the earthquakes and volcanoes that can be destructive from time to time.

In a similar sort of way, a great problem with many illnesses is pain. One thing worth noting about pain is that it is a necessity. It tells us to pull our hand back from a flame. It tells us when we are about to put all our weight onto a foot that is resting on something sharp. It tells us when we ought to get medical attention. Chronic pain may well be an unavoidable 'dark side' of the existence of useful acute pain.

Similarly, the random genetic mutations that allow evolution to take place have the 'dark side' that they can also cause cancers.

There is a type of software program, called a genetic algorithm, which is used in several fields of work. The name, unsurprisingly, comes from the fact that it mimics neo-Darwinian evolution in a limited way.

When a genetic algorithm is used in my field of control systems engineering, one simple approach is to choose a set of parameters (values of various numbers that we can tune) that may result in a system being well controlled but, equally, may not. Then the performance of the system is measured to see how well it is actually being controlled by the use of that set of parameters.

Next, a process analogous to genetic mutation is used, whereby a new set of parameters is generated, by replacing a selection of the original parameters by some randomly generated new ones. Again the performance of the system is measured. If the new performance is better than the previous one, the new set of parameters is kept. If not, the old set is reinstated. The procedure is then repeated, as many times as one wishes, until it is decided that the 'best' performance has been achieved.

Note that the bad performance had to be allowed actually to take place, in order that it could be rejected, in the same way as a bad genetic mutation is rejected by natural selection, because its possessor is less likely to breed successfully.

There are limits to the type of control system to which this approach can be applied (you wouldn't want it to be used in your aircraft's flight control systems), but the point is that the system is allowed to find its own best operating regime. On the assumption that it does so, any intervention by the designer to restrict any bad behavior, reduces the 'space' in which the system is allowed to search for solutions, and will therefore probably lead to a sub-optimal result.

Something similar may well apply in the biological world. The difference between a mutation that potentially produces a good result, and one that potentially produces a bad result can probably be quite small. Possibly, it can be sufficiently small that God could put no preventative mechanism in place without, at the same time, limiting the potential for desirable results.

Since I am not an expert in genetics, this is just speculation on my part. It is correct in the arena of genetic algorithms used in engineering, but it may not be in the real genetic arena of molecular biology. Nevertheless, whatever the details may be, the general principle seems likely to be correct – that it is impossible to have the good mutations without also allowing the possibility of bad ones.

God surely doesn't desire the bad outcomes of any of these things, but perhaps they are an unavoidable part of the way the world works. Perhaps God will not act to prevent such things, but perhaps he will act to bring the best possible outcome from their results, or even, occasionally, to work a miracle, as discussed shortly.

No doubt, as John Polkinghorne says, God will have, "Reserved to himself some providential room for maneuver in bringing about the future of the world."[20] In other words, God can act directly in the world – but in what circumstances?

In terms of our own participation in bringing about changes in the world, Polkinghorne goes on to suggest that, when we pray, perhaps we are cooperating with God in offering him our room for maneuver (in other words our free will) so that he can use it, "In the most effective way in relation to his room for maneuver" to achieve things which are in accordance with his will.

I came across a similar idea some twenty years earlier, in Anne Townsend's book *Prayer Without Pretending*.[106] She corresponded with "a theologian" and asked him why God needed us to pray for God to act in the world, since he must already know what needs to be done.

The theologian replied, "God enables sinful men to enter a little into His creative purposes for the world, to enroll in the struggle (of which the outcome is assured by the resurrection) of bringing His will to be done on Earth as it is in Heaven. Prayer is participating with God in His work, is it not? This is the primary meaning of it all; petition, confession, and even thanksgiving are all subordinate to this. ... Why should God need me to pray? ... he doesn't *need*. But He does *want* my fellowship, my sharing in the work, my constant expression (by the very fact of prayer) of dependence [Townsend's italics]."

Townsend was greatly impressed by the idea that, "God wanted [her] to share in His work throughout the world by [her] praying."

In summary, God has chosen to limit his power and to grant certain freedoms both to humans and to the processes that have led to humans. The overlapping of these freedoms with God's reserved ability to act providentially in the world allows for answers to prayer when we cooperate with God, but not when we pray for things which have already been ruled out by God's own self-limitation.

In praying we give our free will back to God, to use as he wishes. He can then intervene in our lives, because we have given him permission to do so. He can allow us to assist in his actions in the world, and give us the necessary resources to do so. Things will happen when our desires are aligned with God's, because we have freely offered back to him the freedom he first gave us.

## How might God be able to act?

The young children in my church sometimes sing a song that begins:
   My God is so big / So strong and so mighty / There's nothing that he cannot do. ... [107]

That's absolutely fine for children. They will just take it to mean that God is more powerful than a very powerful thing indeed. It is more worrying when adult Christians appear to maintain that it is literally true.

A moment's thought shows that even an all-powerful god, who was free to do absolutely anything he liked, would face some restrictions. As a very simple example, consider a soccer match that took place on the last day of the English football season in 2010. Sheffield Wednesday played Crystal Palace (a London team). Depending on the result of the match, one of the teams was going to remain in their present league, but the other was going to be relegated into the lower division.

Imagine, in Sheffield, a woman whose husband had been suffering from severe depression for many months. As a keen Sheffield Wednesday supporter, he had gone to the match. She was a Christian, and stayed at home praying sincerely for her husband. She thanked God that he was a loving husband and an excellent father to their children, and for all the other good things about him. She thanked God that her husband had felt able to go to the match, and prayed that it would help to raise his spirits.

Then she realized that, were the wrong result to materialize, it would make him feel even worse. She prayed, very sincerely, and for all the right reasons, that Sheffield Wednesday would be successful. She was genuinely thinking only of her husband; for example, the thought of how much better life would be for her if his depression lifted hadn't even occurred to her.

At the same time, imagine, in London, a man whose wife had also been suffering from severe depression for many months. As a keen Crystal Palace supporter, she had gone to the same match. He was a Christian, and stayed at home praying, in exactly the same way, and from exactly the same praiseworthy motives, that God would allow Crystal Palace to remain in the higher league for the good of his wife's health.

You will be way ahead of me by now. However well-intentioned the prayers of those two people were, and even though they were prayed entirely unselfishly and from the best of motives, it was impossible for God to grant them both, in the terms in which they were asked.[108]

Whatever else God may be able to do, he cannot do both of two mutually exclusive things. The children's song could be re-written, by a pedant, as follows:

My God is so big / So strong and so mighty / But some things he just cannot do. ...

But that would spoil the effect of the whole song, and it wouldn't make sense to a five-year old. It's not unusual to introduce simplified versions of ideas initially, and then to refine them as knowledge increases; we do it in education all the time. Leave the song as it is, until the children are older!

However, when we *are* older, we do need to re-think some of our earlier ideas. It was probably already obvious to you that even God cannot do two mutually exclusive things. What is far less obvious is what God, having allowed us free will, will and will not do. Given that God is all-knowing and all-powerful, and yet, if earlier suggestions are correct, he has chosen to self-limit his rights to act in the world, then nobody can really second-guess him. However, although it is tricky, we don't simply throw in the towel at this stage.

It seems likely that if God does act in the world and if we do have free will, then he will at least have to adjust his plans in some sense as time passes. Let's look at this suggestion in a little more detail.

It is often said that God is omniscient (he knows everything). But if we genuinely do have free will, surely he cannot know exactly what we will choose to do next. If he does know, are we not just puppets carrying out pre-determined actions, with no genuinely free choice at all?

So, will we make choices in line with God's will, which allow him to proceed with his 'Plan A', or will we make choices different from his will, which cause him to adopt a less-favored 'Plan B' instead? For example, will he have to rely on someone else to do a certain thing if we choose not to do it?

It has been argued by some that free will is just an illusion, and that God can, in fact, know what we will do next. I don't buy that though, since the whole point of free will is that we must be free to choose to love God, rather than being forced to 'love' him. If that is true, then God, by his own choice, will presumably have to wait and see whether we shall choose to love him or not, and what we shall do as a result.

Perhaps God's 'omniscience' means that he can know all the possible future consequences of all our actions. He can know the consequences which could possibly follow if you, or I, or both of us choose to love him; and also all those which could possibly follow if we choose not to; but he genuinely allows us to select which of those chains of possible consequences actually comes to pass. What we choose is important, and the best choices we can make are those aligned with God's plans.

Similarly, if God does allow the world to make itself, presumably he always knew that creatures capable of loving him and having a relationship with him would arise, because he planned the universe to produce such creatures. But did he know that they would be on Earth, and that they would be precisely what we call human beings? Maybe he did but, if you will excuse the anthropomorphism, it is also conceivable that he may have had a fascinating time seeing how life on Earth 'chose' to evolve in line with his overall plan, and what kind of creatures would appear in the end.

As a very crude parallel to this view of evolution, there are engineering systems that are self-organizing. For example, a 'swarm' of autonomous, mobile, mini robots might be programmed to accomplish some collaborative task. As the task progresses, the result will (hopefully) be of the kind which the designer of the task intended.

However, during the task, each robot makes its own decisions as to how to interact with the others, within the constraints of the task. As a result, the actual path travelled by any particular robot, and the actual actions it takes, can be surprising and unpredictable, even to the designer. Sometimes, if a robot gets stuck, the designer might even have to reach in and help it out of a jam.

Similarly, imagine taking part in an improvised stage play. The writer and director have set up the overall theme and structure of the play, and specified the various scenes that will take place, but the dialogue produced by the actors will surprise even the writer and director from time to time. The director may sometimes have to step in to bring things back on track, if the actors move too far away from the plan.

As suggested earlier, when we say that God is all-knowing, what might be the case is that he knows all possible futures. This is something like the designer of the mini-robot task, or the director of the improvised play, knowing every possible scenario which could ever evolve; or like the ultimate chess grand-master knowing all the moves in every game which could ever be played.

Humanly speaking, these things are impossible. Even in the relatively limited scenarios above, the numbers of possibilities are just too enormous for us to be able to visualize. But if God is omniscient, he can know all possible futures of the universe, even if there is almost an infinite number of them.[109]

If we have free will, or if the universe is free to make itself, then the future must be open; it is not completely determined in advance. God can know all possible futures, but even he doesn't know which of them will come to pass, until it happens.

There are alternative views. For example, it is often pointed out that God is 'outside' time. Assuming that God created time it must be true, because he must exist independently of it. But some then say that, because he is outside time, he can 'see' the past, present and future simultaneously and, to him, the future is as clear as the past is to us.

There is a concept in physics, known as the 'block universe', which fits this idea. In the block universe, all of space and time is taken to exist as a single four-dimensional 'block' in one go. So all of time would then naturally be 'visible' to God, since he would view the block from the outside.

The block universe idea arose from some consequences of Einstein's special theory of relativity, and Einstein himself was a supporter of it. However, there are valid arguments from relativity theory both for and against such a view, and so we must choose whether or not to accept it based on arguments other than strictly scientific ones.

Perhaps I have insufficient imagination (this is quite likely), but I have a problem with any kind of idea that the future can be known in advance. I cannot get away from the feeling that if the future is open (because we have free will, and the universe 'makes itself'), it will therefore be determined by choices we have yet to make, and by chance evolutionary mutations which are yet to occur. In that case, there is no single future yet to be known, only the set of all possible futures. Which of those possible futures will actually come to pass is yet to be determined, by things that have not yet happened.

If we are genuinely free to make choices, and if the universe is genuinely free to make itself to some extent, then I remain unconvinced that the actual future can already be 'out there' in any sense, to be seen, even by a god who exists outside of time.

Of course, another possibility is that we do not genuinely have free will, and also that the evolution of the universe is pre-determined. In that case the problem is removed, because the Creator can know, in advance, the outcomes of all the decisions we shall make, and the details of every other event in creation. However, solving that problem only replaces it by the worse ones that the theology set out in this book is intended to avoid.

For example, I cannot convince myself that I am an actor on a stage, following a pre-determined path, and writing pre-determined lines. I am sure that I didn't *have* to write this sentence.

I am equally sure that I must take responsibility for my own actions. However, if all my actions were pre-determined, that would not be the case. There would be no morality; anything I might do would not be my fault, since I would have no choice in the matter. Law courts, condemning me for any of my actions, would be unfair.

Similarly, if creation is not free to make itself, then presumably God could be held directly responsible for each natural disaster, because he must have pre-planned them all. Many people have pointed out that that would be a good reason not to believe in him.

It is also hard to believe that a loving God would create someone, knowing, in advance, that she is pre-destined to reject him and therefore to be condemned to eternal separation from him (which is what Christians mean by "hell"). In that case, her life would be as meaningless as some atheistic philosophers suggest that it is.

As a final example, nobody would genuinely love God (or anybody else). Whatever their feelings might be, they would not be love if they had no choice in the matter.

This is a tricky area, but the view of God's knowledge of the world as outlined in this chapter, or something similar, is a good candidate for the best explanation of the way things are. It allows us to choose freely to love God, so that our love is genuine, and it gives us the freedom to make life choices that are either good or bad. It is up to us, not to fate, but we, and those whom our choices affect, have to live with the consequences.

How God might then cope with a refusal, on our part, to follow his 'Plan A', is another difficult question. Recall the first few paragraphs of the sub-section headed *What does God have to do with free will?* in the previous chapter. They described the kinds of choices which we might make all the time, but which might end up having life-changing consequences. Now imagine everyone else in the world making similar choices, all the time, with similar chains of potentially important consequences. The resulting worldwide chain-mesh of interrelating consequences is what God has to work with.

For several years, I did the job of timetabling in my part of the University. It was a very complex problem. Amongst other things, there were competing demands from all parts of the University for the barely-sufficient supply of teaching rooms, and competing demands for unique specialist laboratory space from all of the many engineering courses. Added to that were the conflicting availabilities of the various student groups and teaching staff, who needed to come together, in many different combinations, for the various activities. The situation was complicated further by the presence of part-time students and staff, with very limited availability.

I enjoy problem solving, so I was able to cope with that job by treating it as a multi-dimensional puzzle, otherwise it could be a route to an early grave. Even when aided by appropriate computer software packages, it seems to be an occupational hazard that less-fortunate timetablers are prone to suffer from stress-related problems at busy times of the year.

Timetabling is an example of what the mathematicians call a scheduling problem. God seems to have the ultimate scheduling problem to solve, in coping with all the choices of humans, and all the results of the evolution of the universe and of life on Earth, which deviate from what would be his ideal.

As to what God might actually be able to do, it has already been suggested that he cannot have done too many obviously out-of-the-ordinary things, including random miracles all around the world, otherwise the world would not behave in such a regular manner.

However, there is an important difference between God not doing "too many obviously out-of-the-ordinary things" and no action on God's part at all. If there are some direct actions of God going on, some of them might be thought of as miracles, whilst some might be such that we cannot even tell that they have taken place – we shall look at those comments in a moment.

It seems reasonable that God can do some out-of-the-ordinary actions to accomplish things that, for whatever reason, cannot be done any other way. At the same time, such extraordinary events will confirm his presence to those with the faith to see it. There just have to be sufficiently few of them to avoid a descent into disorder, and to avoid sowing seeds of uncertainty about any true laws of nature that we have discovered so far. Also, his actions will be consistent, since he is trustworthy.

Nevertheless, I tend to agree with those who suggest that a lot of what God does in the world may actually be done in ways that are indistinguishable from the normal state of affairs.

I think that God spoke creation into being and that if, at any time, he were to withdraw his will that it should exist, then it would cease to exist. In that case the "normal state of affairs" is actually the result of God's faithful actions, in sustaining his creation in the face of problems which are not of his causing, but which arise from the God-given freedom of people to make their own choices, and of creation to make itself.

As a very simple example, when someone recovers in hospital from a serious disease, or a serious accident, it is usually due to the application of modern medical science and techniques, and the use of modern drugs. The discovery of those techniques and drugs are some of God's blessings to humankind, but that is not the point here. The point is that sometimes, someone who recovers in hospital might actually not have recovered, were it not for the fact that his friends had been praying for him, and God had stepped in, in some way, to aid his recovery.

It may well be impossible for us to distinguish between that, and a 'normal' recovery. It will also be difficult for us to say why the same result did not occur in some other case that, to us, seems very similar. We have to trust that God's much higher level of knowledge than ours would be able to explain that, as was suggested earlier using the example of our cat's unavoidable suffering when she visits the vet.

By way of another example, England tends to have a lot of rain showers, which can happen on any day of the year. If, for some good reason, God were to cause a shower of rain in England by his own direct action, it would often be impossible for anyone to tell whether he had done it directly, or whether it was within the normal range of atmospheric behavior. We shall shortly return to the question of how he might be able do such things.

## Miracles

Still recognizing the difficulties raised above, more obvious miracles may be allowable from time to time. A miracle is something surprising; something that doesn't fit the way we normally expect the universe to work. However, there must also be some very good reason for its having occurred; God is not a celestial magician, who will perform tricks for our amusement.

Some miracles may simply be cases of the operation of laws of nature that we have not yet discovered, but others may really be what they seem – actions of God in the world, which demonstrate his love and providence, to those with eyes to see.

One important point in relation to miracles is that it is incorrect for anyone to say that the laws of nature (or 'of physics', or 'of science') do not permit miracles to occur. In fact, the laws of nature don't permit or prohibit anything at all. They are simply descriptions of how we have observed the world normally to work so far. They have power to predict, but not to allow or disallow.

The occasional miraculous healing is therefore, presumably, allowable, as it won't unduly disrupt the normal course of medical science. Skeptics can dismiss it either as a mistaken diagnosis, or some aspect of medical science that we don't yet understand, or a deliberate deception, or a coincidence.

However, there cannot be enormous numbers of such miracles, for the usual reason: too many would have a disruptive effect on the reliability and consistency of medical science, so that progress in identifying and treating disease would be disrupted.

This kind of idea doesn't demonstrate any lack of faith on my part. I am convinced that miracles (not only medical ones) have occurred in my own life, and amongst people I know. However, I do think that God will be faithful to his general allowance of the world to make itself. I don't think that he will deviate from the laws of nature sufficiently often as to call into question either the laws themselves, or his faithfulness in upholding them.

When religious people claim to have had answers to prayer, especially ones that seem overtly miraculous, atheists will generally claim that those 'answers' are simply coincidences. That, of itself, confirms that what one set of people can interpret as a direct act of God, another set of people can interpret as the normal statistical variation in the operation of the world. In any such cases, God's actions, if that is what they are, are clearly such that they are capable of being confused with normal events.

We shall never know how much freedom God has reserved to himself, to be able to bend the usual ways in which the world operates. Similarly, we shall never know what constraints there may be on his doing so, due to the complex chain-mesh effects of the potential consequences of any actions of his.

Even in cases of non-obvious action, as discussed below, perhaps the constraints on God due to consequences in other people's lives and other areas of the world, which we cannot know about, constitute the reasons why he will act in one case but not in another. Even though the two cases look similar to us, given God's level of knowledge of future possible consequences, they will actually be very different.

An obvious example of a claimed miracle was the resurrection of Jesus. If it happened, then it was clearly something surprisingly unusual. As the skeptics say, "dead men stay dead"; and usually they do. If Jesus were just a man, with no divine attributes, then his resurrection would have been a real shock. If, however, he was God in human form, then perhaps his resurrection was not so surprising – death would not be expected to have any power over him. In fact, if anyone could prove that the resurrection of Jesus did not take place, then I would have to agree with St. Paul's assessment in the Bible that my faith would be futile.[110]

To end this section, since this particular miracle is so vital to Christianity, I shall briefly state some of the evidence for believing it. This version loosely follows the presentation in John Polkinghorne and Nicholas Beales' book *Questions of Truth*.[111]

Firstly, as we saw in Chapter Seven, the relevant biblical records are considered to be very reliable when compared with other historical documents.

Secondly, Jesus' death by crucifixion was the death of a common criminal, so most of those who witnessed it would have despised him. Also, as he died Jesus cried out, asking why God had forsaken him. If the resurrection were a fabricated event, invented to persuade people that Jesus was the Son of God, these would not be impressive details to include in the story.

Thirdly, Jesus was the only founder of a great world religion to have apparently failed. He died young, whereas Abraham, Mohammed and the Buddha all died in old age, with their families or supporters ready to carry on their work. In contrast, the biblical accounts tell us that Jesus' supporters had deserted him and had even hidden themselves away, terrified that the authorities would come looking for them, and with no thought of carrying on his work.

This, apparently, all added up to a dismal failure of Jesus' life and mission, and was not a good basis from which to launch a life-changing faith. As Polkinghorne and Beale point out, if it had really ended there, we should probably never have heard of Jesus.

Something particularly remarkable must have happened to turn all that around. The Bible tells us that Jesus rose from the dead, confirming his status as "The Son of God". That's much more like the basis from which to launch a life-changing faith.

Fourthly, the biblical accounts of the resurrection say that it was a group of women who first reported the empty tomb. This is very strange because, at that time, women were considered unreliable witnesses; they were not allowed to testify in court, for example. Why would unreliable witnesses be chosen to report such a momentous event, unless that is what really happened?

Fifthly, in the various biblical accounts of Jesus' appearances after his resurrection, there is the strange fact that people did not initially recognize him. Since those accounts come from different writers, and describe different events, it is very odd that they all include that strange aspect, which might initially cast doubt on the identity of the risen Jesus – unless, of course, it really happened like that.

Sixthly, in later years, several of Jesus' close disciples were put to death for their beliefs. If they knew that Jesus was dead, and they had been spreading lies and deceit, surely at least one of them would have come clean at the end, confessing that it was all a hoax, and thus saving himself. People do sometimes die for what they believe to be true, but not many are prepared to die for something they know to be a lie. It had to be real; they knew the power of the risen Jesus in their lives.

In addition to such objective arguments, I believe that the resurrection happened because of the experience of the risen Jesus Christ in my own life, and the changes I have witnessed in the lives of others.

## Non-obvious actions of God

If it is correct that we have free will, and that God's creation is allowed to make itself, how might he have kept himself some freedom to be able to act in the world? Are his metaphorical hands now completely tied?

A primary way in which God acts, is through the actions of people who are sufficiently open to his prompting that they are able to discern what they need to do to further his purposes, and sufficiently courageous to do it. The distinguishing characteristics of God's purposes are that they will only increase the levels of such things as goodness, harmony, love, justice and truth in the world. There have been plenty of obvious high-profile examples, such as William Wilberforce, Martin Luther King and Mother Teresa. He can also act through any of us who have chosen to give our free will back to him. In this section though, we shall concentrate on the mechanisms there may be by which God can take direct action in the world.

One possibility is in the counter-intuitive, probabilistic world of sub-atomic particles, as described in the section on *Uncertainty* in Chapter Three. In such an environment, God could presumably do many things that were indistinguishable from the normal behavior of matter. However, since the unpredictabilities generally seem to average out at the everyday scale, it may be difficult to achieve a great deal at the scale of everyday objects by fiddling around with the individual sub-atomic particles which make them up.

Perhaps a more promising field in which God could be at work is that of chaotic systems, described in the section on *Unpredictability* in Chapter Three, which operate at the everyday scale of things, and crop up in all kinds of areas.

Those who belong to the school of thought that says that God must be absolutely consistent in allowing people to have free will, and creation to make itself, might want to believe that he will absolutely never interfere with the physical laws, which he has set up for the universe. If God does have to interfere with those laws from time to time, some would question whether he perhaps made a mistake when he set them up in the first place.

However, given that many natural systems have some chaotic aspects to their behavior, their nature is to be, in some senses, unpredictable. Perhaps God therefore has freedom to inject information, or, indeed, tiny amounts of energy, into such systems, but then to allow them to continue to behave exactly in their natural manner in response to that new information. That seems to be one way in which God can interact with his creation without needing to make any adjustments to the ways in which the laws of nature work.

Personally, I don't find it necessary to go so far as to say that God can *never* interfere in the world's making of itself. That is because it seems that God does sometimes act in ways that go against the usual rules by which the world works. One obvious example is the resurrection of Jesus, as mentioned at the end of the previous section.

Finally, although we still don't understand particularly well how our brains work, it does seem that there is some similar chaotic behavior there too, and therefore perhaps similar freedom for God to act directly on people, in a way indistinguishable from normal events.

In the light of earlier comments, he would only do so in a way that did not affect people's free will. For example, he might perhaps be able to inject information that would cause certain thoughts to arise, but he would not then cause any brain impulses that would predetermine the action that anyone would take in response to that information. That would remain their free choice.

Thus, for example, Hitler may well have had thoughts that he should halt his extermination of Jews, and other people might have been similarly prompted to make that suggestion to him. However, if so, maybe those other people failed to follow up the impulse to say something, for fear of the consequences, and perhaps Hitler exercised his free will to ignore his own thoughts and any suggestions that might have been made by others.

I don't want to stray into the area of brain science here. For an interesting introduction to some of the ideas, in *Questions Of Truth*, Polkinghorne and Beale[111] have a 21-page appendix entitled *The Brain And Mind*. In it they discuss how we handle information, the concept of active information, the fact that the brain has been shown not to be deterministic, whether the mind is separate from the body, the link between the brain and morality, the idea that our free will is probably genuine, and similar matters.

The philosopher Richard Swinburne also has something to say about the relationship between brain and mind in his book *Is There A God*.[112] His thesis is that the existence of God explains the existence of humans.

## Chapter 12  Drawing it All Together

This book has presented some wide-ranging scientific information, albeit at a level of detail limited by the available space.

One of the underlying aims was to suggest, to anyone skeptical of modern science, that they should think carefully about whether well-researched and widely accepted scientific theories can, realistically, simply be denied. To assist in this, various suggestions were made as to how beliefs leading to such denials might be re-considered, without actually having to deny anything fundamental to their faith.

Another aim was to indicate that a deterministic scientific description of the universe, which would completely remove the need for religion, is not a possibility. The uncertainty described by quantum theory, and the unpredictability discovered in chaotic systems at the scale of everyday objects, have removed the possibility of a completely deterministic 'scientific' view of the universe. At the same time, rational justifications have been suggested for many aspects of religious belief.

In parallel with the scientific material, we have also seen several lines of argument, in various areas, which indicate that a great many religious people are actually intelligent and thoughtful. They do not blindly accept the truth of any religious dogma that is presented to them, without evaluating it. Part of that evaluation will be against what the foundations of their religion says, and what we know about God, but part of it will take into account whether it seems to make sense in the light of what we know about the universe.

I admitted, early on, that there would be a Christian bias in the religious aspects of the book. In line with that, the overall aim has been to support my assertion that an authentic religious faith, particularly a Christian faith, need not be in conflict with any well-researched scientific discovery. There are very many good scientists who are also genuine religious believers. It is perfectly rational to be both.

It has also frequently been pointed out that we all live by faith. We all take for granted many basic aspects, both of life and of science, which cannot be proved. More specifically, religious people live by faith that God is reliable, faithful, loving and good, and wants a relationship with them. But scientists also live by faith – for example, that the laws of nature are consistent and can be applied everywhere, that the fundamental constants of nature have values which apply everywhere, and that those laws and constants were somehow 'already' in place at the beginning of space and time, and can be applied to all situations from the big bang until now.

Although we can neither prove nor disprove the existence of God by logical argument, throughout this book we have come across several pieces of evidence for his existence. Many of these pointers towards the existence of God are connected with 'scientific' aspects of the universe, though some are not. For convenience, the final section draws some of these together, since they have appeared in a rather piecemeal way throughout the book.

Before that, here are a few of the questions which we have encountered, and which require answers if we are to have a full understanding of why the universe is the way it is. All these questions really do address the *why*, as opposed to the *how* – the *purposes*, as opposed to the *mechanisms*.

Why is there something, rather than nothing? Why did the big bang occur? Why were the tiny density fluctuations in the early universe exactly of the kind which would lead to the present universe, containing us? Why were the required fundamental constants of nature 'already' built in at the beginning of everything? Why did the laws of mathematics, physics and logic 'already' exist at the big bang? Why are we able to understand the workings of the universe, both by analyzing observations, and by simply thinking about it? Why does the string of coincidences exist which (only just) allows carbon, essential for life, to be formed in stars? Why do the coincidences exist which (only just) allow nuclear fusion reactions to proceed to produce the other elements in stars? Why is Earth positioned in exactly the right zone, relative to The Sun, to support life? Why do the many other 'anthropic', fine-tuning coincidences exist? Why is the behavior of the universe so consistent and reliable that we seem to be able to assume that the laws of nature, which we discover, will apply everywhere; hence we use them to make predictions of things that we expect might be discovered in the future, and also to analyze distant (and hence very old) worlds? Why are non-scientific notions such as beauty, meaning, morals, purpose, truth and values fundamentally important in our daily lives?

Science does not address any of these questions. Those who will only accept explanations that are scientifically verifiable by repeatable tests will have to settle for an incomplete explanation of the universe, because they have to leave these, and other fundamental questions, unasked.

Religious people, on the other hand, have rational answers to such questions. The existence of God answers them all, for reasons which I have outlined in this book. Furthermore, these are not 'god of the gaps' arguments – because these are not the kinds of question which science is suited to answer, there are no gaps here which science will eventually fill.

The closing sentences of the eminent scientist Robert Jastrow's book, *God and the Astronomers* [113] are relevant here. Jastrow was talking about the scientists' dream of explaining the big bang, and musing on the fact that science doesn't seem to have the ability to get right back to the very beginning. The quotation below is from 1992, but the intervening decades have only confirmed that he was right. Here's what he said:

"It is not a matter of another year, another decade of work, another measurement, or another theory; at this moment it seems as though science will never be able to raise the curtain on the mystery of creation. For the scientist who has lived by his faith in the power of reason, the story ends like a bad dream. He has scaled the mountains of ignorance; he is about to conquer the highest peak; as he pulls himself over the final rock, he is greeted by a band of theologians who have been sitting there for centuries."

Talking of theologians, we have also mentioned, almost 'in passing', the existence of some very old arguments for the existence of God, pre-dating modern science by several hundred years. Anselm's definition of God as, "That than which nothing greater can be conceived," still seems an acceptable one.

The medieval approaches of Anselm and Thomas Aquinas, to 'proofs' of God's existence, weren't strict proofs in the modern logical sense. However, they are helpful in forming a rational foundation for thinking about God's existence, especially when re-formulated by modern philosophers.

For example, it was suggested that Alvin Plantinga's reworking of Anselm's 'proof' of God's existence, does at least prove that belief in God is a rational belief to hold. Also mentioned was Keith Ward's suggestion that Thomas Aquinas' 'proofs' can, in suitable circumstances, "provide good reasons for accepting that ... there is a God."

## Drawing it all together

So far, in this closing chapter, we have briefly reviewed some of the fundamental questions which science cannot answer; and will not be able to answer in most cases, notwithstanding the 'god of the gaps' trap. However, if we accept that there is a God who desired that creatures should come into existence, who could have a relationship with him, then that belief leads to answers to them all, perfectly complementing the scientific description of the universe.

We have also looked at some non-scientific reasons for belief in God, including the moral law which, it seems to me, God has placed within us all, independently of the norms of our cultures or societies. In fact, much of what is good in the life of our societies, such as health care and education, grew out of our knowledge of the moral law, and from the work of people who were followers of God.

I am reluctant to suggest that God was directly responsible for 'potentially scientific' things that we still don't understand, such as the mechanisms of the big bang itself, the appearance of the first life, the appearance of self-consciousness, or the mechanisms by which the fine-tuning of the universe might have come about. That's because science may, eventually, discover those mechanisms, without any necessity for God's direct participation. A faith founded on those reasons for belief in God would then fail.

It also seems clear that the normal behavior of the world, which we observe from day to day, is consistently regular, otherwise science could not analyze, explain and predict it. If the behavior of the world were entirely unpredictable, because God often did things, on a widespread scale, which didn't fit those normal patterns of behavior then, by definition, science would be unable to explain or predict it. In fact, science would not be possible.

On the other hand, if we are prepared to believe that there are purposes behind the kinds of mechanism which science investigates, such as those not-yet-understood mechanisms mentioned above, then any questions about those purposes are of are a different kind. They are answered by personal explanations, which address the types of question that are complementary to science. Those purposes are the results of God's choices, and there are no repeatable scientific tests that could be done to verify any hypotheses about choices that God might make.

The next few paragraphs re-state my own position in summary. Everything here is supported by discussions earlier in the book.

There is sufficient evidence to make the existence of God the best explanation for the way things seem to be. He exists independently of our notion of time, and he desired that creatures would exist who would be capable of having a loving relationship with him.

He created the universe by setting up the appropriate initial conditions, fundamental constants and laws of nature for the big bang to occur about 13.7 billion years ago. Since then, he has maintained these rules of nature and the appropriate values of the fundamental constants, faithfully and reliably, and continues to do so today. If he withdrew his support, the universe would cease to exist.

In the meantime, the universe has been allowed to make itself, within the constraints set up by God; a process that has resulted in the existence both of Earth and of us. It has resulted in the intricacies of particle physics and molecular biology at one end of the size scale, and the cosmos as a whole at the other end, and we are those creatures who can have a relationship with their Creator.

Since he wants us genuinely to love him, God has given us free will; it has to be our deliberate choice to invite him into our lives. Misuse of our free will leads to much of the suffering in the world; the rest is the unavoidable 'dark side' of a creation which is allowed to make itself, but which has more benefits than disadvantages.

God has reserved the capacity to be able to interact with his creation, but he will not do so in surprising (miraculous) ways sufficiently often to upset our ability to be able to rely on his faithful laws of nature, which he has also given us the ability to discover for ourselves. He can act in my life, or in yours, only if we pass our free will back to him, to use as he sees fit, with our full permission.

There cannot be a logical proof either for, or against, the existence of God. Our discussions have also indicated that there is no logical problem with holding either the belief that there is a god, or the belief that there is not. Clearly, only one of those beliefs can be correct. If any of us chooses to base our life on the wrong answer, then there will be consequences in this world and, if it exists, in the next. Getting it right could be the most important decision any of us ever makes.

In November 1974, I decided to pray a prayer admitting that I had followed my own way, rather than God's, resolving to turn that around, and inviting God into my life to enable me to do so. Although I didn't immediately realize it, my life has never been the same since. I have seen, and experienced, much to confirm my belief in God, though it would probably not convince determined skeptics who have not experienced it for themselves.

I have given a few pointers to God's existence from my own experience, such as the fact that I feel that I was guided towards a relationship with him once I seriously started looking. I have known many prayers that seem to have been answered over the years. You may put the answers to people's prayers down to coincidence but, as William Temple, an Archbishop of Canterbury in the early 1940s, once remarked, "When I pray, coincidences happen."

Then there is the deep, underlying peace that I have. I also sometimes get a very strong sense of when I ought, or ought not, to take some particular course of action, to the extent that I am extremely likely to follow it. Over the years, this has cost me in terms of convenience, time, money, turning down at least one job offer, and generally going against my own wishes at the time. However, I am sure that the benefits have far outweighed the costs.

I also used to have quite a bad temper when I was younger. I'm sure I was growing out of it by the age of 22, but whatever remained of it immediately vanished when I became a Christian. As one indicator of that, whilst working in industry I attended a three-week residential management course. It was an intensive course that didn't allow participants to go home at the weekends, and kept up a high level of competition between groups and individuals, presumably with the (possibly misguided) aim of helping participants to cope with pressure.

At the end of that course, we had to write critiques of each other. One person simply wrote of me, "He has no temper." On that particular course, that particular person saw me (rightly or wrongly) as the only one who had managed to 'hold it all together' for the full three weeks. He even asked me what made me different from the others – so I told him about the work of Jesus in my life. I ought to add that this was over 30 years ago and that, sadly, my behavior since then has rarely prompted anyone else to ask me such a question!

Similar testimonies from friends, some much more dramatic than mine, result in God's actions in people's lives being, for me, one of the strongest reasons for belief in him.

I have also witnessed extreme suffering and unpleasant terminal illness amongst Christian friends and family, but I have seen God's power at work in the people affected. It has given them a firm hope of the future with him, which is far more valuable than anything which purely intellectual argument, or atheism, can promise.

# Endnotes

1. I chose to alternate between the male and female genders in this book. In places, that sequence has been interrupted by revisions. If your gender seems to get a rougher deal than the other, it is the result of pure chance!
2. God, if "he" exists, is a spirit, and hence beyond gender. I can't bring myself to call God "it" so I shall use the male gender, but without any implication of maleness.
3. If you doubt it, just think of the things that won't work without electricity, such as compressors for the gas supply, pumps for the water supply, pumps to get fuel into vehicles of all kinds, and all the electrical equipment in homes, industry, commerce and hospitals, including all the communication systems. After a while, nothing would work anymore. The food supply and clean water would run out, and you can guess the rest.
4. Stannard, R., *Science and Belief: the Big Issues*, Lion Hudson, 2012.
5. Such a theory will probably need to marry up relativity and quantum theory, but this is proving difficult.
6. As Mark Twain's schoolboy suggested in *Following the Equator*.
7. As the White Queen claimed to be able to do in Lewis Carroll's *Through The Looking Glass*.
8. At the time of writing, the latest estimate was 13.82 billion years, but those results were still being analysed.
9. Manser, M.H. (Ed.), *Collins Bible Companion*, Collins, 2009.
10. Wilkinson, D., *The Message of Creation*, IVP, 2002. (*The Bible Speaks Today* series.)
11. Plantinga, A., *God, Freedom and Evil*, Eerdmans, 1974 (not particularly easy reading).
12. MacKay, D.M., *The Clockwork Image*, IVP, 1974.
13. Thomas Aquinas, *Summa Theologica*, available for reading on-line if you have the stomach for it. The Five Ways can be found in Part 1, Question 2, Article 3, *Whether God exists*.

As one example, try http://www.ccel.org/ccel/aquinas/summa.toc.html (last accessed 22.5.14).

[14] Ward, K., *Why There Almost Certainly is a God: Doubting Dawkins*, Lion, 2008.

[15] As quoted by Alister McGrath in:

McGrath, A., *Dawkins' God: Genes, Memes and the Meaning of Life*, Blackwell, 2005.

[16] Lennox, J.C., *God's Undertaker*, Lion, 2009 (with reference to Nigel Cutland).

[17] Watson, D.C.K., *My God is Real*, Falcon Books, 1969.

[18] This assumes that adult fingernails grow 1mm in one million seconds (just over eleven and a half days).

[19] $10^{-10}$ uses the scientific notation for very small numbers. $10^{-1}$ means 1/10, so it is 0.1, similarly $10^{-2}$ means 1/100, so it is 0.01

A pattern emerges in which the $n$ in a number such as $10^{-n}$ tells us in which decimal place to write the "1". One millionth, 0.000 001 is therefore $10^{-6}$. Similarly, one billionth, 0.000 000 001 is $10^{-9}$. Therefore, $10^{-10}$ means 0.000 000 000 1 which is one tenth of a billionth.

Without this kind of notation, the incredibly short time interval of $10^{-32}$ second, which we shall encounter later, would have to be written as 0.000 ... twenty-six more zeros ... 001 second.

[20] Polkinghorne, J., *Quarks Chaos and Christianity*, Triangle, 1994.

[21] This version of the model has been reduced to the simplest form that demonstrates the required behaviour for our purposes; actual models used to predict populations are more involved.

The equation is $P_{next} = F.P_{now}.(1 - P_{now})$, in which $P_{now}$ represents the population now, $F$ is the factor (just a number) which fixes the dynamics, and $P_{next}$ then tells us the population at the end of the next time interval (let's say one year in the future).

In this very simple model, the population variables ($P_{now}$ and $P_{next}$) are scaled such that 0 means no animals, and 1 represents the maximum number there can be. So 1 might represent 20 animals if we are talking about the population of a large predator in some particular geographical area, or 1 might represent millions if we are talking about insects.

Because $P_{now}$ and $P_{next}$ lie in the range 0 to 1, the term $(1 - P_{now})$ actually represents the difference between the population now, and the maximum value it could be (as limited by the maximum food supply, for example).

To use the equation, choose a value for $F$ (say $F = 2$) and set $P_{now}$ somewhere between 0 and 1 to represent the present number of animals. The equation then gives the value of $P_{next}$, which tells us what the population will be one year in the future.

Next, imagine we have moved forward in time one year. It is therefore necessary to set $P_{now}$ to the value of $P_{next}$ that we have just calculated. Now apply the equation again, to calculate the new value of $P_{next}$, which tells us what the population will be at the end of the next year – and so on.

You cannot do this by hand, because life's too short – millions of iterations around the calculations are necessary to demonstrate the effects described in the text, and the next endnote.

[22] Most of the action can be observed for values of $F$ between 3 and 4. If you try this on a computer, using the model in the previous endnote, be prepared for some very long execution times, as $F$ must only be increased by a very tiny fraction between one run and the next in order to tie down the values at which the changes in behaviour (known as bifurcations) occur. It is entirely understandable that these phenomena were not well investigated before the advent of modern computing power.

[23] Gleick, J., *Chaos: The Amazing Science of the Unpredictable*, Vintage Books, 1998.

[24] The minimum requirements for a system to have the potential for chaotic behaviour are that the system has *feedback* and is *nonlinear*. Feedback means that information from the output of the system is fed back to the input, forming a closed loop around which information flows. Feedback is present in almost all control systems, for example, since a measurement of the system's present output is usually fed back for comparison with the desired output. The amount of error in the output is then used in calculating the required correction to be applied to the input of the system, so as to bring the value of the output nearer to the desired output. In the population example of this section, the value $P_{next}$ is the output of the system, and it is fed back into the model by then using it as the input $P_{now}$ when the equation is evaluated for the next time interval, as described in the earlier endnote.[21]

*Nonlinearity* (at its simplest) implies that the output of a system does not necessarily change by the same factor as the input. For example, in a linear system model, if the input is doubled, then the steady output will also double. In a nonlinear system this may not be the case.

In the population model example of this section, if the right hand side of the model equation is multiplied out, a term $(P_{now})^2$ appears. Therefore, because the value of $P_{now}$ gets squared, if $P_{now}$ were to double, that term will increase by a factor of 4, rather than the factor of 2 expected in a linear model.

[25] Venus has a very reflective atmosphere (which is why it is so bright) and so it exhibits phases of alternating illumination and darkness (in the same way as The Moon does) as the relative positions of Venus, Earth and The Sun change.

[26] Strictly speaking, the red-shift effect in receding galaxies is not due to the Doppler shift, but rather to the expansion of space (to be described shortly), which effectively stretches the light waveform as it is on its way to us, thus lowering its frequency. However, the conclusion is the same.

[27] The oscillation is due to an unstable interaction between the pressure from nuclear reactions at the centre of the star (tending to expand it) and gravitational attraction (tending to collapse it). The time period of each cycle of oscillation of such a star might be just a day or two, but some have periods of several weeks.

[28] This is done by comparison with the known brightness of The Sun, and the known distance of The Sun from Earth.

[29] The idea that time began at the big bang may seem very strange. It is a consequence of Einstein's relativity theories. Before Einstein, we thought of space as having the usual three dimensions (length, width and height for example), and we thought of time as being something completely independent. Einstein showed that speed, space and time are all closely intertwined. For example, as speeds become very high, lengths contract and clocks run slower – both of which have been shown to be true by experiment. Since Einstein, because we now know that space and time are so closely linked, we have to think of the universe as a four-dimensional space-time environment. It then seems more natural to suggest that, if space came into existence at the big bang, so did time.

[30] Davies, P., *The Goldilocks Enigma: Why is the Universe Just Right for Life?* Penguin, 2006.

[31] Recently (in Penrose, R., *Cycles of Time: What Came Before the Big Bang?* Vintage Books, 2011), the eminent mathematician (and cosmologist) Roger Penrose has suggested that the accelerating expansion of the universe might be interpreted as the "big bang" of a new universe.

This harks back to a previous idea that our "big bang" might have been part of a cycle of expanding and re-collapsing universes, though the discovery of the accelerating expansion of the universe seemed to have ruled out that suggestion.

Penrose's book contains other intriguing suggestions that are outside the mainstream of current scientific ideas, including a suggestion that the current theories of the inflationary[37] period of the very early universe may be "misconceived". As always, Penrose's ideas are very interesting, but I can't tell whether they are likely to be the beginning of a new theory that will become generally accepted.

You will find Penrose's book hard going, unless you have a higher than average knowledge of mathematics and physics.

[32] Barrow, J.D., *The Origin of the Universe*, Basic Books, 1994.

[33] $10^{32}$ (pronounced "ten to the power thirty two", or usually just "ten to the thirty two") means thirty-two 10s multiplied together. It is the same thing as a one followed by 32 zeros. It follows exactly the same pattern as numbers you already know, such as the fact that $10^2$ is 100, whilst $10^3$ is 1,000. Similarly, $10^6$ is one million (1,000,000), $10^9$ is one billion or a thousand million (1,000,000,000), and $10^{12}$ is one trillion or a million million (1,000,000,000,000).

It is actually pretty meaningless (even to scientists) to write out the number 100,000,000,000,000,000,000,000,000,000,000. Similarly, expressing it as one hundred million trillion trillion doesn't help much either, so $10^{32}$ is a very convenient shorthand.

Even if you have understood all that, it remains a meaningless number! Later, when talking about the number of stars in the universe, I'll use a little trick which goes some way towards helping to visualise such numbers, but this one is really too large even for that.

[34] The "K" stands for "Kelvin", which is a unit of temperature. A *change* of temperature of one Kelvin is exactly the same thing as a *change* of temperature of one degree Celsius, so if your room temperature rises by 4°C, it also rises by 4K. In other words, the sizes of the Kelvin and Celsius degree are identical.

The difference between the two scales lies in where 0°C and 0K are placed. Any particular temperature expressed in Kelvin is simply 273.15 degrees greater than the same temperature measured in °C. So, if your body temperature is 37°C, it is also 310.15K. Zero K (so *minus* 273.15°C) is known as 'absolute zero', and is the coldest temperature possible. At 0K all molecular motion ceases and no heat can be extracted from anything.

[35] The Large Hadron Collider is one of our most complex engineering achievements. Look up the CERN website to be impressed by further details. http://home.web.cern.ch/topics/large-hadron-collider (last accessed 23.5.14).

[36] The highest temperature achieved in LHC collisions at the time of writing (only fleetingly, of course) is about 5.5 trillion K. That sounds pretty hot and, indeed, it is about 365,000 times hotter than the centre of The Sun. Nevertheless, it is 'only' $5.5 \times 10^{12}$K, so it needs another 19 or 20 zeros adding onto the end before it reaches the temperature of the big bang. Compared with that temperature, 5.5 trillion K is completely negligible.

[37] That may sound impossible, but it isn't. The speed of light is, indeed, a speed limit for anything travelling *through* space. However, what we are talking about is the expansion *of space* itself, not the speed of something moving through space. Relativity theory doesn't describe any speed limit for the rate of expansion of space itself. In McGrath, A.E., *A Fine-Tuned Universe*, Westminster John Knox Press, 2009, Alister McGrath states that the universe initially increased in size by a factor of $10^{35}$, in $10^{-32}$ second[19], ending up roughly the size of a grapefruit. Expanding from virtually zero, even to the size of a grapefruit, in such a very short time, would comprehensively break the normal light-speed barrier.

This brief period is known as the inflationary stage in the development of the very early universe. After it, the rate of expansion returned to its normal (sub light-speed) value.

[38] The number of protons is unique to each element, and is known as the atomic number of that element. For example, carbon has six protons, and an atomic number of six. If an atom does not have six protons, it isn't carbon.

Every normal element is electrically neutral. The proton has a positive electrical charge, the neutron has no charge, and the electron has a negative electrical charge, equal in magnitude to the positive charge of the proton. So a normal atom has as many electrons as protons.

The number of neutrons in a normal atom is not quite so easy to specify. For normal carbon atoms, it is the same as the number of protons, six. The mass number is defined as the sum of the number of protons and the number of neutrons, thus carbon-12 is a normal carbon atom with six protons and six neutrons. Changing the number of neutrons gives a different isotope of the same element, which has different properties. For example an atom of carbon-14 must still have six protons because it is carbon, but its mass number is 14, so it has eight neutrons. This is the radioactive type of carbon, whose decay into an isotope of nitrogen is used for radiocarbon dating.[51]

The number of neutrons in a normal atom can be found from the well-known periodic table of the elements, as follows. Look up the element in such a table, and its atomic number is normally given at the top of its cell in the table. In the case of lithium, as an example, find the cell for Li near the top left of the table. The number at the top is its atomic number, three, so any lithium atom has three protons. At the bottom of the cell is usually a number called the atomic weight, which depends on all the possible isotopes of the element. In the case of lithium it is 6.94. Now round this to the nearest whole number, and you get the mass number which, for lithium, is therefore seven. With a mass number of seven, and three protons, a normal lithium atom must therefore have four neutrons.

Using the same method for hydrogen, with an atomic number of one and an atomic weight of 1.008, the number of protons is one, but the mass number is also one (1.008, rounded to the nearest whole number) so there are no neutrons. A normal hydrogen nucleus is therefore just a single proton (orbited by a single electron).

[39] Rees, M., *Just Six Numbers*, Weidenfeld and Nicholson, 1999.

[40] Ironically, at the time Penzias and Wilson made their accidental discovery, a facility was actually under construction, elsewhere, to mount a formal search for the microwave background radiation.

[41] Available at http://hubblesite.org/gallery/album/pr1995044a, with descriptive notes. Last accessed on 25.11.13.

[42] Despite its name, a light year is a measurement of distance. It is the distance travelled by light in one year. Since the speed of light is 299,792.46 kilometres per second, one light year is about 9.46 trillion kilometres, that is 9.46 million million kilometres, or $9.46 \times 10^{12}$ kilometres. If you prefer imperial measurements, the speed of

light is 186,282.40 miles per second, making a light year about 5.88 trillion (5.88×10¹²) miles.

[43] Cox, B. and Forshaw, J., *Why Does E = mc²?* Da Capo Press, 2009.

[44] Some think that the source of these small variations may have been the random fluctuations that are described, by quantum theory, as happening all the time, and everywhere. They are generally only important at sub-atomic scales, so they would have been much more significant in the very early universe, when everything was extremely close together, than perhaps they generally are now.

The idea is that random quantum fluctuations may have had the effect of causing some areas to expand slightly more than others in the inflationary period of the very early universe,[37] and hence to become slightly less dense than others and, as a result, to emit slightly less radiation than denser areas occupying the same volume of space.

[45] If you look at the images from the Hubble Space Telescope on the world-wide-web, you will find several pictures of nebulae shaped like rings of one sort or another. Some of these are the results of stars exploding as supernovae, and the rings are the ejected gas and dust containing all the manufactured chemical elements. Whatever might remain of the original star will probably be invisible, somewhere near the center of the ring.

[46] Estimates of the number of stars in the Milky Way vary; 200 billion is at the lower end of the scale and some estimates are twice that number. It is difficult to come up with an accurate number because we cannot see them all. Clouds of gas and dust obscure many parts of the galaxy, so we must calculate the likely number of stars based on estimates of galactic mass, and luminosity measurements.

[47] To be more precise, I am imagining of a sphere 62.035mm in diameter, so its volume is 125,000 cubic millimetres, and each cubic millimetre contains eight of my salt grains, giving a total of one million.

[48] If you are sufficiently sad as to be crosschecking my arithmetic, don't forget that a year has 365.25 days on average.

[49] According to Newton's law, gravity attracts every mass to every other mass, with a force proportional to the two masses involved in any particular case, and inversely proportional to the square of the distance between them. So, the greater the masses involved, the greater is the gravitational attraction; the farther apart the masses are, the weaker is the attraction; as the separation increases, the attraction reduces rapidly.

[50] Two objects are attracted to each other by the electromagnetic force if one has a positive electrical charge and the other has a negative electrical charge; or if one is a south-seeking magnetic pole and the other a north-seeking magnetic pole. Conversely, this force causes two objects to repel each other if they both have the same type of electrical charge, or the same magnetic polarity.

[51] That is how the decay of a carbon-14 atom to nitrogen, mentioned earlier, occurs.[38] A carbon-14 atom has six protons and eight neutrons. As a result of the behaviour of the weak nuclear force, one of the neutrons eventually emits a couple of tiny particles, and becomes a proton, resulting in the seven protons and seven neutrons of normal nitrogen. The half-life of Carbon-14 is about 5,730 years, meaning that, on average, half of an original quantity of carbon-14 will decay to nitrogen-14 in 5,730 years.

[52] In stars whose mass is much less than that of The Sun (one tenth, for example), the temperature in the core may still reach several hundred thousand degrees, but that is not hot enough to fuse hydrogen nuclei into helium. Such a star gives out radiation due to the heat at its core, but never properly 'ignites' and is known as a brown dwarf.

Stars with less mass than The Sun, but more mass than a brown dwarf, are often of lower density than The Sun. Such a star might be, for example, one third of the Sun's mass but twice its diameter. The core of a star like this will also reach several hundred thousand degrees. However, after several hundred million years of gravitational contraction, perhaps to a quarter of the Sun's size, the higher gravitational compression due to the greater mass, results in core temperatures of perhaps five to 10 million degrees, so that hydrogen can fuse to helium.

According to the book *Stars*,[56] it is thought that such a low-mass star, known as a red dwarf, may continue to shine for up to 30 billion years, eventually converting all its hydrogen fuel to helium and then ending up as an inert ball of helium known as a black dwarf. The universe is not yet old enough to verify this.

[53] A normal beryllium-9 atom has five neutrons.

[54] If you want to look up further details, the reaction resulting in carbon is often known as the 'triple-alpha' process, because an alpha particle is a helium nucleus, and three of them are involved in this process of carbon production – though not in one simultaneous collision.

55 In comparison, stars with similar masses to The Sun do not become dense enough or hot enough to do this. Instead, they undergo a few other phases of stellar life including, after billions of years, a period as a red giant, which, in the case of The Sun, will engulf Mercury, Venus and probably Earth. Eventually, such stars shrink and end up as hot, dense, white dwarfs, with most of the chemical elements they have manufactured remaining inside them.

56 *Stars*, Voyage Through the Universe series, Time-Life Books, 1988.

57 DNA is the acronym for deoxyribonucleic acid.

58 In the case of animals which rear their young, a 'successful' animal actually has to survive a little longer than the time at which it gives birth, in order to ensure that its offspring survive to the stage at which they can care for themselves.

59 Lennox, J.C., *God's Undertaker*, Lion, 2009.

60 See, for example, Polkinghorne, J., *Science and Creation: the Search for Understanding*, SPCK, 1988.

61 Collins, F., *The language of God: a Scientist Presents Evidence for Belief*, Simon and Schuster, 2007.

62 McGrath, A., *Dawkins' God: Genes, Memes and the Meaning of Life*, Blackwell, 2005.

63 http://www.nature.com/scitable/topicpage/dna-packaging-nucleosomes-and-chromatin-310. Last accessed on 27.11.13.

64 Note that this retains all the original information. If a section of mRNA contains the sequence A, G, A, U, C, given that the possible pairings are fixed, and that U has replaced T, the original DNA sequence must have been A-T, G-C, A-T, T-A, C-G.

65 Two bases selected from A, C, G and U, with the four possibilities for each one, could code for only 16 different amino acids (AA, AC, AG, AU, CA, CC, CG, CU, etc.). Three bases (AAA, AAC, etc.) could code for 64 amino acids, but redundancy between the codes results in the production of one of only twenty possibilities for any of the three-letter codes. The *Nature* web-site http://www.nature.com/scitable/topicpage/nucleic-acids-to-amino-acids-dna-specifies-935 (last accessed on 27.11.13) contains a table showing the results of the possible combinations.

66 Dawkins, R., *The Ancestor's Tale: a Pilgrimage to the Dawn of Life*, Weidenfeld and Nicolson, 2004.

67 Dawkins, R., *The God Delusion*, Bantam, 2006.

68 Experiments along these lines have been carried out in laboratories, and have succeeded in producing amino acids after only a few days. But they have failed to produce anything resembling the complexity of DNA or RNA, or anything at all self-replicating in the sense that life is. Perhaps, given the few hundred million years between the formation of the atmosphere of the early Earth, and the appearance of life, they might do so; but that is by no means a certainty.

Another suggestion for the origin of life involves the chemically rich environment around hydrothermal vents in the oceans. In this case, the required energy would obviously not come from lightning strikes, but perhaps from an electrical 'battery' resulting from the electrochemical gradient between alkaline water in the vent, and acidic water in the surrounding ocean, with the structure of the vent providing a semi-permeable membrane in between. This is similar to the mechanism by which the mitochondria within cells provide the energy required to keep you going. However, again, nobody really has much idea as to how the first life could have formed in such an environment.

69 Dawkins, R., *The Blind Watchmaker*, Penguin, 1986.

70 Dawkins, R., *The Greatest Show on Earth: the Evidence for Evolution*, Bantam, 2009.

71 If something is described as "irreducibly complex", it will be something that can only function with all its parts present. The implication is that it could not have evolved by small gradual changes, as all the parts would then not have been present. Quotations such as, "What use is half an eye?" or "What use is half a wing to an insect?" are often seen. But biologists such as Dawkins maintain that no example has yet been found for which a gradual evolutionary process cannot be suggested (apart from the origin of the very first life).

72 I am interpreting the creation story in Genesis 1:26-31 as telling us that God created a man and a woman on the sixth day, and then the story in Genesis 2:7-25 as saying that they were Adam and Eve, and that what is reported in those verses of Genesis Chapter Two also took place in the Garden of Eden on the sixth day of creation. Personally, I don't think that everything that this approach describes as having happened on the sixth day could actually be crammed into a single day, but we'll let that pass.

73 1 Corinthians 3:19.

74 David Wilkinson mentions this, as do Michael Green and Nick spencer, in their book,
Green, M. and Spencer, N., *I'd Like to Believe But...*, IVP, 2009.
75 Pearce, E.K.V., *Evidence for Truth, Volume 1 – Science*, Eagle, 1998.
76 Wilkinson has a PhD in astrophysics, as well as one in theology, and I know that this throwaway line about the stars struck him even more forcibly than it struck me.
77 John 1: 1-14.
78 This "John" was John the Baptist, not John the writer of the gospel.
79 See Chapter 10 of Wilkinson's *The Message of Creation*.[10]
80 John 8:12.
81 "In the beginning" which opens John's gospel, is a direct quotation from the opening words of the book of Genesis, so this is to be understood as being concerned with creation.
82 See, for example, Bruce, F.F., *New Testament Documents: are they Reliable?* IVP, 1981.
83 As found in, for example, *The Complete C.S. Lewis Signature Classics*, Harper Collins, 2007.
84 Despite the fact that Lewis wrote *Mere Christianity* to summarise a set of radio broadcasts which he presented 70 years ago, it is worth reading that book for his full arguments on this topic, though his style, and some of his comments, are very obviously '1940s' these days.
85 Polkinghorne, J., *Science and Christian Belief*, SPCK, 1994. An excellent book, but not necessarily easy reading.
86 *In Memoriam*, Alfred Lord Tennyson, 1850.
87 The "herd instinct" is here being used as a description of the desire to adopt forms of behaviour that benefit all members of society, rather than the individual.
88 To take an anthropocentric view of something is to assume that it happened for the benefit of humankind. It is very easy to do unthinkingly, and the term is often used, in a slightly disparaging way, in connection with those who don't realise that they are doing it.
89 There are microorganisms on earth which have survived at -80°C in laboratory tests, and also ones which live at +110°C near hot thermal vents on the ocean floor. Humans could not have evolved in such extremes though.

[90] See the Kepler Space Telescope website at kepler.nasa.gov for more details. In the spring of 2013, the KST suffered a malfunction that, at the time of writing, seems to have halted its search for planets orbiting other stars. However, it is hoped that the KST is still sufficiently operational to be put to other uses instead.

[91] Barrow, J.D. and Tipler, F.J., *The Anthropic Cosmological Principle*, Oxford, 1986. You may find this huge book hard going in places, but it does contain a lot of detail relevant to chapters eight and nine.

[92] Viewed from a long way away, Earth would be seen to wobble from side to side, because of the gravitational attraction of The Moon as it orbits Earth. Because the mass of Earth is about 81.3 times the mass of The Moon, the centre of mass of the system comprising Earth and The Moon is only $1/81.3 = 0.012$ of the distance from the centre of the Earth to the centre of The Moon. The resulting point is about 4,730km from the centre of the Earth, which is actually inside Earth. Thus, The Moon is actually orbiting a point inside Earth, located 4,730km along the line joining the centre of Earth and the centre of The Moon, whilst Earth also 'orbits' the same point, with Earth's centre always on the opposite side of that point from The Moon; hence the 'wobble'. Many pairs of stars orbit each other in binary systems, and each star in such a binary pair orbits about the pair's shared centre of mass in the same way.

[93] Hawking, S., *The Universe in a Nutshell*, Bantam, 2001.

[94] In fact, Einstein introduced this constant in order to allow him to *remove* the tendency of his equations to predict either the expansion or contraction of the universe, since it was thought, in the early 20th century, that the universe was static. When the expansion of the universe was discovered, Einstein said that this had been, "The greatest blunder of [his] life".

[95] Mark 12:30.

[96] According to John Polkinghorne,[97] Augustine apparently had the notion, in the fourth or fifth century, that, "The initiating timeless act of creation brought into being the 'seeds' from which eventually a multiplicity of different creatures would develop in the course of a process of temporal germination." To me, this is suggesting that Augustine thought that God set up some suitable initial conditions, and that the development "of different creatures" was somewhat autonomous after that.

[97] Polkinghorne, J., *Exploring Reality: the Intertwining of Science and Religion*, Yale, 2005.

[98] Polkinghorne, J., *Science and Creation: the Search for Understanding*, SPCK, 1988.

[99] Kingsley was a friend of Darwin's, and was also a keen naturalist. If you can find an early edition of his classic book *The Water Babies*, published in 1863 (four years after Darwin's work), although it is notionally a children's book you will find that it contains several evolutionary references, including comments on some of the controversies of the time. Unfortunately, more recent editions seem to have been 'dumbed-down' by editing out most of Kingsley's scientific comments and asides, leaving only the basic story line. As a guide, a 1908 edition that I have seen still contained the original material (incidentally, it would have been an extraordinarily bright child who could appreciate everything in the original version!)

[100] McGrath, A., *A Fine-Tuned Universe*, Westminster John Knox Press, 2009.

[101] As one example, in *The Greatest Show on Earth*,[70] Richard Dawkins describes, in detail, how a certain parasitic wasp lays its eggs inside live caterpillars, and the intricate lengths to which it goes to make the process successful – from the wasp's point of view, not the caterpillar's. The details are fascinating, but it might be preferable not to be eating when you read them, if you are squeamish.

[102] A book by Douglas Spanner, *Biblical Creation and the Theory of Evolution*, Paternoster Press, 1987, is one that mentions this sort of idea.

[103] See, for example, Richard Leakey, *The Origin of Humankind*, Weidenfeld and Nicolson, 1994. Also note that there would have been other female humans around at the time. If the "Mitochondrial Eve" theory is correct, it means that none of the other females gave rise to lines of descent that led to anyone who is alive today.

The mechanisms for correcting mutations in the DNA in mitochondria are not as effective as those in the nucleus, so mitochondrial DNA is also subject to more mutations than 'normal' DNA (in the nucleus), which makes it even more useful for tracing lineages back in time. In addition, because there are so many mitochondria in each cell, mitochondrial DNA is easier to find in remains from long ago.

[104] See, for example, Deuteronomy 33:27 (first half), Psalm 89:8-9, Proverbs 16:33, John 5:17, Ephesians 4:10, Colossians 1:17,

Hebrews 1:3 (first half) and Hebrews 1:10-12, to mention but a few. I present these references without further explanation. For that, you will also need to find a bible commentary, or a bible with copious footnotes and cross-references, such as a study bible. If this area intrigues you, I also recommend David Wilkinson's book *The Message of Creation*,[10] in which he studies the theme of creation running through the whole of the Bible.

[105] Ward, K., *Divine Action*, Templeton Foundation Press, 1990.

[106] Townsend, A., *Prayer Without Pretending*, Scripture Union, 1973.

[107] Ruth Harms Calkin, Nuggets of Truth, 1959-2002.

[108] The match was drawn. As a result, Crystal Palace stayed in the upper league, whilst Sheffield Wednesday went down to the lower division, because Wednesday had needed to win. The match, and the result, really happened, but the two prayers were invented as an illustration.

[109] It is a good job that God is a spiritual being, otherwise the professional engineer in me would have to ask how all this knowledge could be stored!

[110] See 1 Corinthians 15:14.

[111] Polkinghorne, J. and Beale, N., *Questions of Truth: Fifty One Answers to Questions about God, Science and Belief*, Westminster John Knox Press, 2009.

[112] Swinburne, R., *Is There a God?* Oxford University Press, 2010.

[113] Jastrow, R., *God and the Astronomers*, Norton, 1992.

# Index

## A

Absolute temperature scale · 50
Adam and Eve · 141
Age
   of Earth · 17, 92
   of Universe · 12, 46, 93
Alpher, Ralph · 52
Anselm · 19, 165
Anthropic principle · 66, 113, 164
Anthropocentric viewpoint · 116
Aquinas, Thomas · 22, 165
Argument from Design · 87, 116
Aristotle · 22, 23, 41
Atheism · 132, 169
   faith required for · 8, 19
Atom, empty space · 51, 64
Augustine · 23, 53

## B

Bacon, Francis · 2
Barrow, John · 50, 122
Beale, Nicholas · 158
Behe, Michael · 73
Bible · 136, 143, *Also see* Genesis
   as a library · 13
   reliability · 102
Big bang · 12, 14, 45, 47, 90
Block time · 153
Block universe · 153
Butterfly Effect · 35

## C

Cancer · 147
Cells · 75

Chaotic systems · 34, 39, 160, 163
   air molecules example · 37
   pendulum example · 35
   population dynamics example · 37
Christian
   becoming one · 26, 168
Chromosome · 78
Clockwork universe · 29
COBE satellite · 53
Collins, Francis · 2, 77
Commandment
   greatest · 133
Concert, example of reductionism · 20
Constants · *See* Universal constants
Control system · 16, 111, 130, 147
Copernicus, Nicolaus · 2, 41
Cosmic microwave background · 52, 58
Cosmological constant · 127
Creation · 91
   big bang · 12, 14, 45, 47, 90
   dates · 13

# D

Dark energy · 48, 125
Dark matter · 125
Darwin, Charles · 71, 72, 88, 139
Davies, Paul · 47, 53, 124
Dawkins, Richard · 83, 85, 89
Density variation, early universe · 59
Design argument · 87, 116
Determinism · 32, 163
Deterministic system · 30, 32, 39, 163
DNA · 75, 77
Doppler shift · 44
Dynamic systems · 29, 34

# E

Eagle Nebula · 55
Early universe · 12, 49, 58, 116, 125
Earth
   age of · 17, 92
   magnetic field · 113, 147
   molten outer core · 147
Earthquakes · 138, 147
Einstein, Albert · 6, 42, 48, 127, 153
Electromagnetic force · 64, 123, 124

Engineering · xv, 23, 29, 31, 35, 147, *Also see* Control system
Evolution · 5, 14, 23, 71, 91, 97, 138, 139, 141
   description · 72
   examples · 71
Expansion of the universe · 45, 118, 125
Explanation, personal · 13, 21, 24, 74, 167

# F

Faith · 7, 9, 163
   of atheists · 8, 19
   of scientists · 8, 9, 10, 116, 131, 165
   of the author · xvi, 9, 16, 17, 28, 104, 158
Fine-tuning of the universe · 111, 119, 164
Free will · xii, 131, 134, 145, 151, 160
Fundamental constants · *See* Universal constants
Fundamental forces · 64
Future, open · 75, 152

# G

Galaxy · xi, 43, 44, 56, 57, 61, 93, 117
   cluster · 57, 59, 128
   rotating · 59
   super cluster · 57
Galileo · 2, 41
General relativity · *See* Relativity
Genes · 72, 80, 83
Genesis
   book in the Bible · 12, 91
   genre · 14
   interpretation · 14, 95
   not a science text · xi, 14, 54, 98
   personal explanation of creation · 14
Genetic algorithm · 147
Genetic mutation · 71, 72, 88, 147
God · *Also see* Jesus
   acting in the world · xii, 3, 17, 149
   all-knowing · xi, 151, 152
   all-loving · xi, 25, 137
   all-powerful · xi, 25, 138, 150, 151
   Anselm's definition · 19, 165
   as Mind behind the universe · 21, 32, 55, 74, 77, 86, 115, 130
   encounter with · 10, 25, 26, 142
   no proof, for or against · 8, 164, 167
   of the gaps · 22, 29
   omnipotent · *See* God, all-powerful
   omniscient · *See* God, all-knowing

Gödel, Kurt · 24
Goldilocks zone · 120
Gravity · 5, 12, 42, 64, 113, 123, 125
Greatest commandment · 133

# H

Habitable zone · 120
Half-life · 33
Heisenberg, Werner · 33
Helium
    proportion in universe · 51
Hell · xii, 154
Heredity · 71
Herman, Robert · 52
Hillis plot · 83
Hot oven example · 11
Hoyle, Fred · 48, 66
Hubble Space Telescope · 55
Hubble, Edwin · 44
Hubble's law · 45, 93
Humason, Milton · 44
Hydrogen · 51
Hypothesis · 4

# I

Inflation of the universe · 175, 176, 178
Interesting questions · x, 164

# J

Jesus · *Also see* God
    encounter with · 98, 168
    historical · 102
    mad, bad or God · 102
    resurrection · 103, 149, 157, 160
    suffering · 103

# K

Kelvin temperature scale · 50
Kepler Space Telescope · 122
Kepler, Johannes · 2, 24, 42, 93
Kingsley, Charles · 139

# Index

## L

Lamaître, Georges · 47
Laplace, Pierre-Simon · 42
Large Hadron Collider · 50, 176
Large numbers · 50, 175
Laws of nature · xi, 8, 18, 54
   there at the beginning · 54
Laws of science · *See* Laws of nature
Lennox, John · 24, 73
Light
   light year · 56
   speed of · 8, 56
Lightning · 137
Lorenz, Edward · 35

## M

Machine-mindedness · 32
MacKay, Donald · 32
Mathematical model · 30
McGrath, Alister · 77, 139
Mendel, Gregor · 71, 79
Messenger RNA · 81
Microwave background radiation · 52, 58
Milky Way · 45
   size · 56
Mind of God · 21, 32, 55, 74, 82, 86, 130
Miracles · xii, 131, 148, 155, 156
Mitochondrial DNA · 76, 141
Model, deterministic · 30, 38, 163
Moon, The · 121, 122
Morgan, Thomas Hunt · 79
Mutation, genetic · 71, 72, 88, 147

## N

Natural disasters · 138, 147, *Also see* Earthquakes, Volcanoes
Neo-Darwinism · 72
Neutron star · 56
Newton, Isaac · 6, 32, 42
Nothing buttery · 19
Nuclear force
   Strong · 64
   Weak · 64, 68
Nucleosynthesis · 51

## O

Open future · 75, 152
Oven, heating example · 11

## P

Paley, William · 86
Pendulum, chaotic · 35
Penzias, Arno · 52
Personal explanation · 13, 24, 74
    of creation in Genesis · 14
    sometimes the most relevant · 21, 167
Pillars of Creation · 55
Planck Surveyor satellite · 53
Plantinga, Alvin · 19, 166
Plato · 22
Polkinghorne, John · 37, 75, 105, 139, 148, 158
Population dynamics, chaotic system · 37
Prayer · xi, 3, 75, 131, 145, 150, 157, 168
Proof · 15
    definition · 17
    examples of difficulty · 18
Providence · 148, 156
Pulsar · 56

## Q

Quantum theory · 33, 127, 163
Questions, interesting · x, 164

## R

Red shift · 43
Reductionism · 19, 39
Rees, Martin · 51, 124
Relativity
    general · 6, 42, 48
    special · 153
Resonance
    in carbon atom · 67
    pendulum · 67
Resurrection of Jesus · 103, 149, 157, 160
Revelation · 101

# S

Satellite
  COBE · 53
  Planck Surveyor · 53
  WMAP · 53
Science
  applied · xv
  faith required for · 8, 9, 10, 116, 131, 165
  laws of · *See* Laws of Nature
  may not be the most important explanation · 21, 167
Scientific method · 4
  in theology · 9
Scientific notation
  large numbers · 50, 175
  small numbers · 37, 172
Scientism · 32
Shakespeare · 13
Slipher, Vesto · 43
Small numbers · 37, 172
Socrates · 22
Sound waves, example of reductionism · 20
Space telescope
  Hubble · 55
  Kepler · 122
Speed of light · 8, 56
  exceeded by expansion · 176
Stars · 12, 59
Strong nuclear force · 64
Suffering · xi, 24, 103, 132, 136
Supernova · 69

# T

Temperature scale · 50
Theology, as science · 9
Theory of everything · 8
Time
  beginning of · 12, 47, 49, 53, 90
  block · 153
Tipler, Frank · 122

# U

Uncertainty · 29, 159, 163
Universal constants · 8, 112, 164

Universe
  age · 12, 46, 93
  allowed to make itself · 54, 75, 137
  block · 153
  clockwork · 29
  density variation · 59
  early · 12, 49, 58, 116, 125
  expansion · 45, 118, 125
  scale of · xi
Unpredictability · 29
Ussher, James · 13

# V

Very large numbers · 50, 175
Very small numbers · 37, 172
Volcanoes · 138, 147

# W

Ward, Keith · 22, 145, 166
Weak nuclear force · 64, 68
Weather systems · 35
Wilkinson, David · 14, 91, 99, 101, 185
Wilson, Robert · 52
WMAP satellite · 53

Made in the USA
Charleston, SC
03 September 2014